FORGOTTEN RECIPES

FORGOTTEN RECIPES

From the Magazines you Loved
and the Days you Remember

Compiled and Up-dated
By
Jaine Rodack

Published by

WIMMER
B·O·O·K·S

WIMMER
B·O·O·K·S

First Printing 1981
Second Printing 1983
Third Printing 1985
Fourth Printing 1989
Fifth Printing 1990
Sixth Printing 1991
Seventh Printing 1992
Eighth Printing 1993
Ninth Printing 1994
Tenth Printing 1995
Eleventh Printing 1997
Twelfth Printing 1998
Thirteenth Printing 1999
Fourteenth Printing 1999
Fifteenth Printing 2000

Compiled by: JAINE RODACK
Cover Design: Ken C. Hagenback
Edited by: Ann Upshaw
Cover Illustration: Dickey L. Stafford

International Standard Book Number – 0-918544-60-2

Printed in the USA by
WIMMER
The Wimmer Companies
Memphis
1-800-548-2537

For additional copies, use order forms in back of book or call
The Wimmer Companies
1-800-727-1034

In Memory of
my parents, Rose and Samuel Rodack
My Grandmother, Ida Miller
My Uncle, Joseph Miller
and my second mother, Rebecca Rodack

JAINE RODACK

ABOUT THE AUTHOR

YOU HEARD HER TALK SHOW ON THE AIR
HER JINGLES WERE PLAYED EVERYWHERE
SHE WROTE AND SPUN A DISC OR TWO
CREATED ADS AND VOICED THEM TOO.

FOR FUN SHE BOUGHT OLD MAGAZINES
BROWN AND TORN TO SMITHEREENS.
FIRST SHE BOUGHT THEM FOR THEIR ADS
THEN SHE READ THEM FOR THEIR FADS
KEEPING THEM FOR RECIPES
(THOSE LONG FORGOTTEN MEMORIES)!

NOW SHE'S PUT THEM IN A BOOK
ON THE CHANCE YOU'LL LOOK AND COOK.
FOR IT REALLY WOULD BE ROTTEN
IT THEY WERE AGAIN, FORGOTTEN.

(AND ALL HER WORK HAD BEEN FOR NOTTEN).

INTRODUCTION

It all started out simply enough. I went to a flea market and bought an old, yellowed magazine from the 20's. When I got it home, I realized what a treasure I had! Not only were the articles a bit of living history, but the entire magazine was a look at the way people of the day kept house, shopped and cooked. There were fashions, commentaries by leading authorities, and readers' letters expressing their views.

From then on, I was hooked. I bought, lived, and breathed magazines. The artwork was—breathtaking. The stories—terribly romantic, and the recipes—sensational!

I re-discovered some things I hadn't eaten for years and came upon others I'd never heard of, like Timbales and Rinktum Diddy.

After many years, I have finally assembled some of these recipes, and put them together so that others might enjoy them. Depending on the year they were written, their instructions differ greatly. In the late 1800's there were no controlled ovens and recipes said "cook til done." Fireless cookstoves and other now-forgotten inventions varied instructions as well. So you may have to experiment a bit to get the heat and cooking time straight. I tried to keep them as close to the original recipe as possible. There are also household hints to try or marvel at, and bits and pieces of memorabilia to let you know what was going on at the time these recipes appeared.

ENJOY!

TABLE OF CONTENTS

Yesterday's Kitchens

Yesterday's Kitchens

What would we do without our blenders, electric ice-cream freezers, mixers and food processors? We're extremely fortunate to be able to enjoy the recipes of yester-year with the convenience foods and helpers of today. Imagine going to your local blacksmith for your cook forks and pot hooks . . . having him personally make your dippers, and toasters. In years gone by everything had to be well-thought out ahead of time—there was no running to the local store to buy a carrot peeler or two. Tinsmiths made most of the smaller cooking items, coppersmiths made the saucepans, pots and kettles. Oh, there were some peddlers around in those early days—carrying housewares on their backs, but about the only sign I still see of this fellow is the broom man who comes into my neighborhood every so often.

Although many things were purchased, many more were actually made at home. Women made their own brooms, brushes, and doormats. In the Pennsylvania Dutch areas people had bread troughs which held the flour for them . . . butter paddles and so on.

As kitchens became modernized, items we think of as "new" came into being. As a collector of old magazines I can browse through turn-of-the-century advertisements for dishwashers and "fireless" cookstoves of all kinds. The fireplace with its ratchet-hanger and pots disappeared from the market, or was made ornamental with the advent of ovens. Some fireplaces had built-in ovens and ranges built in to them as times changed. These were built in over their own fireboxes, while a portion of the fireplace remained open. By the 1900's most people had some sort of cookstove, and by the 1920's recipes were available with degree specifications instead of the here to fore "cook until done."

People bought cabinets complete with flour sifters and sugar bins . . . with table-top-sized splatter ware work spaces, and lots of shelf room. The woman of today, complete with her wall to wall built in kitchen cabinets, use these pieces as interesting antiques. But in the early 1900's they were necessities.

It is interesting too, to find new products introduced to American housewives. Things we take for granted as always having been there . . . desserts like Jello-O, which had to be explained to the housewife . . . . And not-that-much-later-than-you-think, instant coffee. Sometimes these new ideas were too far ahead of time, and had to be re-introduced at a later date. Dishwashers made many appearances before becoming a part of our everyday life. Bran cereals appeared, and then disappeared, only recently returning to our grocery shelves . . . for their fiber content.

Roam through the pages of yesterday's magazines and see how economists helped you live on 26 cents a day . . . cope with choosing a new house for $5,000 . . . and modernizing your kitchen with beautiful marble linoleum.

Yesterday's discoveries are today's nostalgia. Don't you wonder what future generations will find collectable? Some day your new electric ice-cream freezer may be worth a lot more than you paid for it . . . as an antique!

INFLATION

THEN AND NOW
A LOOK AT INFLATION

In 1949 an article appeared in a leading magazine. The subject: the cost of feeding a family of three. According to this article, you could feed such a family on $10 a week . . . and feed them well. For $10, you could bring home enough groceries to provide the following week's menu:

potato soup	green pepper strips
beef liver	carrot-bacon-egg sandwiches
molasses sweet potatoes	beef stew
buttered kale	molasses cookies
sliced bananas	macaroni and cheese
egg sandwiches	creamed hamburger

12

vegetable-bean soup
applesauce
fish
bologna sandwiches
eggs au gratin
milk at every meal
meatloaf
baked potatoes
green beans
custard

mashed potatoes
cabbage salad
prune whip
bean soup
scalloped potatoes
cabbage-green pepper salad
bread and margarine at every meal
hot cereal for breakfast every morning
fruit juice for breakfast every morning
creamed potatoes

While I could not figure an exact cost (seeing as how most of us have some seasonings and basics such as mayonnaise already on our shelves) I decided to see how this $10 cost figure measured up to today's prices. This is what I found:

margarine	1.05 a pound
orange juice	3.19 for 2 quarts
two loaves of bread	1.80 (90¢ per loaf)
a gallon of milk	2.65
one box hot cereal	1.07 (Quaker Oats)
can of bread crumbs	.79 a can
green beans	.79 a pound
box of custard mix	.69
10 pound bag of potatoes	1.78 (Idaho potatoes)
3 pounds of liver	1.47 (49¢ a pound)
3 pounds sweet potatoes	.87 (29¢ a pound)
kale (I substituted spinach)	.41 (4 boxes frozen spinach for 1.64)
4 bananas	.50 (25¢ a pound)
one dozen eggs (LARGE)	.79
vegetable-bean soup	.67 for a 10¾ oz. can
applesauce	.63 for 15 oz. jar
fresh fish (8 oz. each person, or 1½ pounds)	2.54 (catfish, at $1.69 a pound)
bologna	2.49 a pound
cheese for macaroni	1.39 for 8 oz.

cheese (grated) for eggs	.61 for 3 oz.
green peppers	2.07 for three
carrots	.39 for a small bag
bacon	2.69 for one pound, sliced
stew meat (2 pounds)	1.40 ($.70 a pound)
molasses	1.39 a jar
flour	.69 for two pounds
macaroni	.49 for 8 oz. bag
ground beef (3 pounds)	2.85 (.95 cheapest available)
head of cabbage	.97 (average head seemed to be 2½ pounds, at 39¢ per pound)
box of prunes	1.23 for one pound box, unpitted

TOTAL SPENT IN 1983 FOR
   $10 WORTH OF
   GROCERIES IN 1949 . . . . $41.58

*In 1978, these groceries totaled $33.49. This is an increase of 25% in just 5 years.
*This is an increase of 320% since 1949 when they cost just $10.00.

Household Hints

Household Hints

Household hints (many suggested by readers) have been a part of America's magazines for over 90 years. Though some of these ideas have been replaced by new-fangled polishes and remedies, I thought you might like a sampling of the household hints of yester-year.

Include a box of paper clips in your sewing basket. You can snap them on to a long seam and save basting. Clipped to a certain needed part of a pattern, it will be there when wanted. Samples to be matched with other fabrics will be ready when clipped to a shopping list. And SEW on.

Mix three pounds of margarine with one pound of butter and see if your family can tell it from four pounds of butter.

When you have pieces of cheese that are too small to grate, push them through your potato-ricer. Likewise, when you have new potatoes which are too small to peel, boil them, and then push them through a ricer. The skins will not go through, and you can butter the riced potatoes and serve them with salt and pepper.

Paint leftover clothespins white, and initial them with nail polish or the like; make one pin for each member of the family. Then use them in the bathroom to keep the towels of the different members of your family separated.

If your child wears bloomers, and has trouble putting them on the right way, work the front button hole with colored thread. That way the child can tell the front from the back.

Clean a lantern chimney by placing a bag (brown paper, preferably) over your hand, and wiping the chimney clean.

Protect your fingernails when gardening by scratching soap under them. This will keep the dirt out, and can be easily removed with a nail brush and hot water.

To get the cloud out of heavily polished furniture, wipe it with a cloth wrung tightly out of warm water to which one tablespoon of vinegar has been added, and polish with a soft, dry cloth.

A 1935 reader suggested that you add some vinegar to the water you use to dampen your pressing cloth. Use this when pressing woolen things, and they will look fresher, and keep a crease longer. Just remember to use ¼ cup of vinegar to one basin of water.

Here's a trick for the kids. Monogram handkerchiefs, bureau scarves, and luncheon sets without touching a needle. Draw your design with some wax crayons, and press the back of the cloth with a hot iron. The heat draws the color through the cloth, and permanently stamps the decoration. It won't run, fade, or wash out.

If you don't want to spend money on dress shields, use four thicknesses of tissue paper, cut in a shield shape, and pin this to your dress.

To clean your jewelry use a little soap on a soft brush that you have dipped in amonia and water. After washing in this solution, rinse in cold water, dry on an old handkerchief, and rub with a chamois skin.

Have trouble sleeping? I found this suggestion in a 1918 magazine: Before you go to bed, eat a good sized raw onion sprinkled with a little salt. You can have a slice of bread and butter along with this, and if it's still a bit much to take, sprinkle the onion with a little lemon juice. You can use the same thing, made into a tonic, for muddy skin. (I would suggest you try this one when you plan on sleeping alone!)

When the original knob on your tea kettle lid comes off, use an empty spool cut in two, and fastened with a bolt and burr.

If you don't have a sewing machine with a lightbulb, use a small flashlight to light up the eye of the needle for threading.

When slicing bacon, always place the rind side flat, and don't try and slice through it. When you've cut what you need, slip the knife under them, and you can slice them easily.

Warm seedless raisins, and drop them into hot, strained honey for "a honey of a sandwich spread."

To keep a sick-room from smelling like a hospital, pour lavender water in an old plate. Light and burn this. You'll find that as it burns it gives off a refreshing odor to the room. If you can't find lavender water, this 1922 reader suggested you burn sugar or coffee grains on a hot stove lid, or shovel (she must have had a coal stove!)

Have radiator heat? Place a metal bread box over it and use it as a warming cabinet for your dishes. This works nicely if your radiator is in the dining room, where you can keep your foods hot while eating. In the summer use this same cabinet as a cooler, by putting it in an ice chest, where a kitchen or camping area is not equipped with a refrigerator. (a 1916 contribution).

To preserve olives after you have opened a bottle or can, cover them with olive oil, vinegar, and salt, and they will keep perfectly fresh.

Clean a rusty stove top by brushing it well with kerosene when it's cold, and letting it stand for half an hour. Then rub and wipe with soft paper towels. Give it a second application, and let it stand, and then rub with steel wool. (1925)

When the weather outside is so cold that your butter won't soften up, try this trick. Pour hot water into a bowl, and let it stand for a few minutes. Empty the bowl, and turn it upside-down over the butter. It will soon be soft enough to use easily (Not the bowl, the butter!)

Save lemon peels and when you need them, soften them by placing them in the oven for a few minutes.

To renovate velvet which is matted and creased, stand a hot iron on end, and cover the bottom of it with a wet cloth. Hold the wrong side of the velvet next to the cloth. You can use the steam from a tea kettle too. (1926)

Give your windows an alcohol rub in the winter when water would freeze. This also prevents the window from steaming up.

Get a first-aid box together in an old cigar box. Include band-aids, sterilized gauze, adhesive tape, an antiseptic wash, a small pair of scissors, and a jar of salve. Let your older children know where it is so that they can learn to use the box themselves. If they are too young to help themselves, keep the box handy, so that you can get to it faster, should you need it.

Trying to use less sugar? During the war years these substitutions were necessary. Now they give you a choice.
Use gingerbread with apple sauce which has been sweetened with syrup
or
Gingerbread with whipped cream sweetened with honey
or
Bread pudding sweetened with syrup and served with marshmallow sauce

Try apples baked with honey or syrup, and stuffed with raisins and nuts
or
Brown Betty sweetened with syrup and served with one of the syrups you will find in this book.

Sweeten your custards and puddings with honey

How about sliced oranges with sweet coconut?

Pumpkin pie sweetened with sorghum . . . .

or molasses cookies served with fruit sauces and sweetened with syrup.

Breakfast

Breakfast

1922 PORK SCRAPPLE

Being from Pennsylvania, we're famous for our scrapple. I'm personally not much of a scrapple eater, but it's worth trying if you're tired of the same thing every day for breakfast. You'll need:

1½ pounds pork shoulder	2 teaspoons salt
1 quart cold water	⅛ teaspoon pepper
1 cup corn meal	

Cut the pork into small pieces, and crack the bone and put it all into a large kettle. Now add the cold water and cook until the meat is tender. Remove the bone, and measure the liquid that remains. Add enough water to make it one quart. Now heat it to the boiling point, and stir in the corn meal. Add your salt and pepper, and cook for 2 hours more. As you cook this you'll see the meat turning into shreds. When your two hours are up, turn this mixture into a greased pan. Cool, and when ready to use, cut into one third inch slices, and sauté. No other fat is needed.

1928 GRIDDLE CAKES (PANCAKES)

Just try and find a house, even a pre-fabricated one sans lot, for $548 today. I dare you! Back in 1928, ads ran in many magazines featuring such a bargain that included 5 rooms, a porch, AND—a bath. Helmets of something called "grosgrain" were the style. They were sexy little hats that looked somewhat like the helmets you see in Prince Valiant comic books. This recipe was first published in that year, and lends itself to many variations. The basic recipe calls for the following:

2 cups flour	2 tablespoons melted
½ teaspoon salt	shortening
3½ teaspoons baking powder	2 egg whites, stiffly beaten
1½ cups milk	1 teaspoon vanilla or other-
1 beaten egg	flavored extract (optional)

This recipe will make about 2 dozen cakes, according to how big you pour them.

To make griddle cakes, mix and then sift all of the dry ingredients into a bowl. Add the well-beaten egg to the liquid. Add the liquid mixture to the dry ingredients very gradually, and stir quickly. Now add the melted fat, butter or oil, egg whites, and at the very last, the flavoring.

Hint: A piece of bacon rind is the best fat for greasing a griddle. *Hint #2:* Turning a cake more than once makes it tough!

Variations on the basic griddle cake recipe:

Cereal Griddle Cakes:
Substitute half a cup of cooked cereal for half a cup of flour in basic recipe. Oatmeal is a good hot cereal to use!

Nut Griddle Cakes:
Add ¾ cup of chopped nuts or nuts and raisins to basic recipe.

Cheese Griddle Cakes:
Add half a cup of grated cheese to basic recipe and serve with tomato sauce for lunch.

Sour Milk Griddle Cakes:
Substitute 2 cups of sour milk for 1½ cups sweet milk to basic recipe, and substitute one teaspoon of baking soda for one teaspoon of baking powder.

1931 WAFFLES

Things were looking up for the 1931 consumer. Washing machine manufacturers had come up with something called an activator, which ended the bunching up and tangling of clothes. People were drinking postum instead of coffee-: Why even the kids could drink it and feel grown-up. Waffles filled many a breakfast dish, and one enterprising young food editor thought up a bunch of exciting new recipes to try on the old waffle iron. These are just some of them:

For the Basic Recipe You'll Need:

2 cups flour
4 teaspoons baking powder
½ teaspoon salt

2 eggs
1¼ cups milk
⅓ cup melted butter

Sift and measure your flour, and then add the dry ingredients and sift again. Now beat just the egg yolks and add them to the milk. Stir the liquid ingredients into the dry ones, and add your melted butter. Beat your egg whites until they are stiff, and fold them into the batter just before baking. Bake in your preheated waffle iron for 2 or 3 minutes. Make sure the iron is nice and hot. Increase your milk if the batter is too thick.

Feel Adventurous? Try these variations to the Basic Recipe.

Cheese Waffles:
Reduce butter to 2 tablespoons and add ½ cup grated cheese. Fold in the cheese last.

Bacon Waffles:
Add 4 slices of uncooked bacon which has been cut into small pieces. Sprinkle the bacon over the batter after it has been poured in the waffle iron. Try this recipe using cooked bacon if you prefer.

Ham Waffles:
Reduce your butter to 3 tablespoons and add ½ cup of cooked ham (chopped). Fold in the ham last.

Nut Waffles:
Add ½ cup chopped walnuts or pecans. Fold in nuts last.

Corn Flake Waffles:
Reduce your flour to 1½ cups, and add a cup of finely crushed corn flakes and 3 tablespoons of white corn meal. Reduce your milk to one cup, and add the sifted dry ingredients.

Date or Raisin Waffles:
Add a cup of chopped dates or raisins to basic recipe. Dredge the fruit with 2 tablespoons of the flour in your basic waffle recipe, and then fold in your fruit last.

CORN WAFFLES

2 cups cake flour	2 eggs, separated
4 teaspoons baking powder	1 cup milk
1 tablespoon sugar	2 cups canned corn
½ teaspoon salt	⅓ cup melted butter or oil

Sift your dry ingredients first, and then measure them. Beat the egg yolks, and add the milk. Now stir your liquid ingredients into the dry ones, and add the corn and melted butter or oil. Beat the egg whites until they are stiff and fold them into the batter. Now bake in a hot waffle iron for one minute. Turn off the power and let it sit there for another two minutes (this will vary with your waffle iron). Makes 9 to 10 waffles.

1934 BANANA WAFFLES

This recipe came along a couple of years later. 1934 was the year Melba toast was introduced as Toast Melba, and refrigerators had a new gimmick—they were now hermetically sealed. For this recipe forget the other basic ingredients, or at least the quantities, and go with this:

2 eggs, separated
2 cups milk
⅓ cup melted shortening
2 cups flour

3 teaspoons baking powder
1 tablespoon sugar
½ teaspoon salt
⅔ cup thinly sliced bananas

Beat the egg yolks until thickened, then add the milk and melted shortening to the beaten yolks. Beat egg whites until stiff and set aside. Now sift the dry ingredients together, and add them to the yolk mixture. Fold the beaten egg whites into this mixture; gently stir in bananas. Pour batter into a hot waffle iron. Bake for 3 minutes.

GINGERBREAD WAFFLES

⅓ cup butter
1 cup molasses
½ cup sour milk or
   buttermilk
1½ teaspoons baking soda

1 egg
2 cups cake flour
2 teaspoons ground ginger
1 teaspoon salt

Put the butter and molasses in a pan and heat it until it boils. Remove from the fire and stir in the milk and soda, along with a well-beaten egg. Don't forget to sift the rest of your dry ingredients (it helps prevent lumps) and add them to your milk mixture. Bake in a hot waffle iron for 1 minute, turn off the power, and leave them in the iron for another 2 or 3 minutes. Serve with crushed fruit or whipped cream. Serves 7 to 8.

Breads

Breads

1935 CHOCOLATE BREAD

How quickly we get used to luxury! Can most of us remember a time when we did without air-conditioning? In 1935 fans were cooling our kitchens as we cooked, and most of them were hand-motored. Our kitchens now featured refrigerators with recessed doors no less, for added storage, and flexible metal ice trays. Gas burners lit themselves, and advertisers told the public you could get thousands of lights with one burner. Sounds like we're talking about disposable cigarette lighters doesn't it? Ah, progress.

For this unique bread, first published in 1935, you'll be needing:

1 cake compressed yeast or dry yeast cake	1 well-beaten egg
½ cup scalded and cooled milk (105° to 110° F.)	1 teaspoon melted shortening
	1 cup chopped nuts
3 tablespoons sugar	1 tablespoon vanilla
1 teaspoon salt	1½ to 2 cups flour
	3 tablespoons cocoa

Soften the yeast in lukewarm milk with the sugar and salt; let it stand for 5 minutes. If you use dry yeast let it stand 1½ hours. Now add your egg, shortening, nuts, and flavoring. Sift the flour and then measure it. Now sift that with the cocoa. Add this mixture very slowly to your yeast mixture, beating after each addition. Do this until the dough is just stiff enough to knead. Knead on a lightly-floured board until it is smooth and elastic. It should be slightly softer than bread dough—so knead it for about 10 minutes—maybe a little less. Place the round ball in a bowl, and cover it with a damp cloth. (I use a moist paper towel—one of the heavier quilted variety.) Put it in a warm place and let it rise until it is doubled in bulk. This takes about an hour. If you used dry yeast it would be best to let it rise overnight in a warm place. Otherwise, knead lightly, and form your dough into a loaf. Place this in a loaf pan, brush with oil, and cover again with that damp cloth. Let it rise another hour or until it is again doubled in bulk. Bake in a moderate oven at about 375° (if this seems too slow raise to 400°), for about an hour.

1937 SODA BREAD

I love people who make it their business to predict the future. Some choose the ever-present future—say 6 months or a year from the date. That's kind of risky because people remember. The folks who seldom get caught in their mistakes are the ones who predict what will happen in ten or twenty years. In 1937 a fellow named Norman Bel Geddes predicted these things in a national magazine:

> *By 1960 he felt that local traffic would use full width streets, and there would be no sidewalks. No kidding, Norman? Tisk. He said there would be no parked cars either. I wonder where he thought they'd all go? And Mr. Bel Geddes felt all sidewalks would be elevated, so they wouldn't really be SIDE walks. I caught you Norman!*

Here's a recipe from that same vintage year when the predictors went a little crazy. It calls for:

1 teaspoon baking soda	1 teaspoon sugar
1 teaspoon salt	Flour
1 teaspoon cream of tartar	Sour milk or buttermilk

Combine the first 4 ingredients and then rub them through a sieve. For making white soda bread use ½ of the soda mixture to 1 cup of flour. Then mix as a soft drop dough with sour milk. Pour into a well-greased pan and bake in a 450° oven for 12 minutes. For Brown Soda Bread use 1 cup of whole wheat flour and ½ cup white flour with ¾ teaspoon of the soda mixture, and bake as above.

1927 PEANUT BUTTER BREAD

Although we think of unusual breads as being very modern, you'll find as you look through old cookbooks and magazines that almost nothing is really new. Here's a delicious 1927 recipe for Peanut Butter Bread. Try it spread with orange marmalade or cheese! You'll need:

2 cups flour	⅓ cup sugar
4 teaspoons baking powder	½ cup peanut butter
1 teaspoon salt	1½ cups milk

Sift first 4 ingredients together, and then add peanut butter. Beat the mixture well. Now add milk; beat well. Pour batter into a well-greased bread tin and bake at 350° for one hour. This recipe will make one large loaf, or two small ones.

Household Hints from 1925

Convenient Spool Holder
A very simple but most convenient spool holder is made by cutting a piece of tape to fit the wrist and attaching hook and eye at the ends to fasten. Place a hairpin or small wire at center of tape, run the wire thru the spool, turn back the ends, and your spool will go with you anywhere, and is never in the way.

The Laundry Basket Habit
Instead of a laundry bag I use ordinary bushel baskets, two of them enameled in ivory. One is kept in the bedroom closet and one in the bathroom closet. These require no washing or ironing and the two save me many steps every week. On wash day the clothes are carried to the line in one of these very baskets. Then, when the clothes are "gathered in" I place the starched garments in one basket and the rough ironed in the other, thus saving a special sorting after the clothes are carried into the house. The sprinkled clothes are placed in the basket with a paper above and beneath and no matter how warm the weather they are nice and damp next morning. Once you get the habit you will find the baskets almost indispensable.

Saving the Extra Fish
When the men go fishing and bring in more fish than we care for fried I place some in my pressure cooker and cook for 30 minutes at 10 pounds of pressure. This makes the bones tender as those of salmon. Then I mash the fish, add bread crumbs, 1 egg and salt to taste, shape into patty cakes and fry.

Keeping the Hair Clean
Slip a rubber bathing cap over the hair while sweeping or dusting, for the dust will not sift thru this as it will thru the cloth dust caps. This will be found especially useful when emptying the carpet sweeper or the bag of the vacuum cleaner.

A Feather Container
I made a frame 1 foot wide, 1 foot deep and 1 foot high. I covered it with screen and nailed it to my wash-house wall. Now, when picking a chicken I place the feathers in the container to dry. When dry they are burned or lawn and porch pillows are made from the feathers. This keeps the yard clean and adds to the splendor of the lawn and porch.

Soups

Soups

1918 CREAM OF ONION AND CHEESE SOUP

Grape Nuts celebrated their 20th birthday . . . Nestlés urged mothers not to wean their babies on cows milk with the warning that it was meant for calves and not babies. They were trying to sell mothers a purified and modified version. Hemlines were almost at the ankle, skirts were full, with front ties, dresses were frocks, and checks were in. A dishwasher put out by a firm named Walker promised that it worked (I should hope so), and used electric or hand power. I've had the latter for years—they're attached to my wrists. Anyway, 1918 was also a good year for soup, and you made it on top of your fireless cookstove.

2 tablespoons fat	1 cup grated cheese
4 diced onions	salt
2 tablespoons flour	Pepper
1 quart milk	Paprika

Melt the fat in the kettle and add the diced onions. Cook until brown, then add flour, stirring constantly. Add milk (a little at a time), stirring constantly. When the soup is hot and thickened, add the cheese and stir until it's combined. Season with salt, pepper, paprika, and serve.

1923 GOLDEN SOUP

Like squash? It's so plentiful in the summertime, that it's a shame to waste all that good nutrition. For this easy-to-fix soup you'll need:

¾ cup cooked squash
1 pint milk
1 pint water
2 tablespoons butter

3 tablespoons flour
Salt, pepper
Onion juice

Strain the squash and add the milk and water together with it in a pot. Bring the mixture to the boiling point, and then rub your butter and flour together, and add that to the soup. Cook until the liquid becomes thickened, stirring constantly. Add your salt and pepper to taste, along with a few drops of onion juice.

1926 RICE SOUP

You'll need:

¼ cup raw rice
3 cups boiling water
1 teaspoon salt
1 slice of onion
1 stalk celery, chopped
2 red pimentos

2 cups veal or chicken stock
2 cups cream
⅛ teaspoon white pepper
3 tablespoons butter
3 tablespoons flour
Parsley

Cook the rice in the boiling water, and add your salt, onion and celery. Cook until the rice is very tender. Now add the pimentos and press all of the mixture through a strainer. Mix the veal stock with the cream and pepper. Add the butter and flour which you have creamed together. Bring the mixture to the boiling point, stirring constantly, and serve sprinkled with parsley.

Timbales
and
Chou Shells

Timbales
and
Chou Shells

TIMBALES

Have you ever heard of Timbales? They were very popular in the first half of this century, and even into the early fifties. But somewhere along the way, we lost them. The dictionary tells us Timbales are pastry shells filled with seasoned food. But often times there is no shell, and the Timbales are made in muffin-like pans and come out like muffins of meat or fish or whatever.

The simplest kind of Timbale is made with a custard foundation. You can make all kinds of Timbales if you'll remember to use one egg to each half cup of liquid, and as much seasoned meat or fish as you wish. Remember to grease your timbale molds or miniature muffin tins well, and set the molds in a pan of hot water. Finally, you generally bake Timbales in a slow oven, about 300°. The cooking time depends on the size and consistency of the Timbale. A Timbale cooked in an ordinary custard cup usually requires 30 to 40 minutes baking time.

SALMON TIMBALES

2 eggs	⅛ teaspoon pepper
1 cup milk	1 cup flaked salmon, drained
¾ teaspoon salt	1 pimento, finely chopped

Beat the eggs slightly, just so the yolk and white are mixed. Add the milk which has been mixed with the seasonings. Then add the salmon and pimento; mix well, and turn into timbales molds that have been well-greased. Bake as directed in basic timbale recipe. Serve with tomato sauce, or green peas.

1918 TOMATO TIMBALES
WITH CHEESE SAUCE

In 1918 everyone was buying liberty bonds. Roosevelt was a colonel, and people were converting waste rags into briquettes for their coal stoves. This was one recipe they cooked in them.

3½ cups canned or fresh tomatoes	¼ teaspoon pepper
1 cup corn cut from cob (optional)	2 slices of onion
	4 whole cloves
1 cup water	2 tablespoons sugar
1¼ teaspoons salt	2 eggs
	¼ cup cracker crumbs

Simmer the tomatoes, (corn, if desired) water, and salt and pepper, along with the onion, cloves and sugar for 15 minutes. Rub through a sieve. Add the crumbs and slightly beaten eggs. Pour this mixture into greased timbale molds or miniature muffin cups and bake at 350° for 20 minutes or until firm. Turn out on a platter and pour the Cheese Sauce over them.

Cheese Sauce:

1 tablespoon fat	¼ teaspoon salt
1 tablespoon cornstarch	¼ teaspoon dry mustard
1 cup milk	¼ teaspoon paprika
⅓ cup grated cheese	

Melt 1 tablespoon of fat, then add 1 tablespoon of cornstarch, and mix well. Now add 1 cup of milk, and bring it to the boiling point. Beat well, and add the cheese, salt, mustard, and paprika. Stir until the cheese has melted, and pour over the baked timbales.

GREEN PEA TIMBALES

2 eggs
1 cup milk
¾ teaspoon salt
⅛ teaspoon pepper

1 tablespoon minced parsley
1 cup drained canned peas or
  cooked peas
1 tablespoon minced onion

Prepare these as you would Salmon Timbales (page 41) and serve with tomato sauce. Leftover canned asparagus, spinach, cauliflower and so on also can be used.

SPAGHETTI TIMBALE CUPS

Sometimes, you'll want to make these cups and place the timbales inside them. To do this you'll need:

Uncooked spaghetti noodles
Salmon, green peas, or other
  vegetable

Pimento
Water

Boil the spaghetti whole by first putting the ends in water, and as they become soft they'll bend enough so that you can get them in a kettle without breaking. When the spaghetti is ready, rinse it with cold water, and lay it out straight on a paper towel. Remember to grease your molds, and then coil the spaghetti around the inside of the timbale mold or miniature muffin tins so that it will be like a cup or shell. (This should completely cover the mold.) Fill these shells with salmon, or peas, or your choice of vegetables, and bake according to basic timbale directions. For a touch of glamour, place a little piece of pimento at the bottom of the mold, and when the mold is emptied upside-down, there will be a nice decorative touch.

CANNED SOUP TIMBALES

2 eggs
Your choice of 1 can of split
   pea, asparagus, or tomato
   soup
¼ cup cream or 2 tablespoons
   melted butter

1 pimento, finely chopped
1 small onion, minced
½ green pepper, minced
¾ teaspoon salt
⅛ teaspoon pepper

Prepare these timbales as you would Salmon Timbales, or bake in a casserole. For variety, add a cup of hot tomato purée and then sprinkle with a cup of grated cheese. This should be done right after the timbales are cooked; return to the oven just long enough to melt the cheese.

1945 CORN AND FISH TIMBALES

2 eggs, separated
½ cup milk
2 tablespoons chopped fresh
   parsley
½ teaspoon Worcestershire
   sauce
1 tablespoon melted butter

1 cup cooked fish or shrimp,
   flaked, and cut into small
   pieces
1½ cups cooked or canned
   corn
½ teaspoon salt
Dash of pepper

Beat the egg yolks until thick and lemon colored; add them to the milk along with the parsley, and Worcestershire sauce. Add butter, and mix well. Add the fish and corn; season with salt and pepper. Beat egg whites until stiff, but not dry; fold egg whites into fish mixture. Pour the mixture into greased custard cups; put the cups into a pan of hot water. Bake at 350° one 1 hour. Serves 6. Only 150 calories per serving.

1920 SPINACH TIMBALES

2 cups cooked spinach   ⅛ teaspoon pepper
4 eggs   ⅛ teaspoon paprika
4 tablespoons melted butter   ½ cup milk
1 teaspoon salt

Rub the cooked spinach through a coarse sieve. Then beat your eggs just slightly; add the melted butter, seasonings, and milk to eggs. Add the spinach. Pour the mixture into a greased baking dish, ramekins, or pyrex glass custard cups, and place in a pan of hot water. Bake in a slow oven (325°) til firm. Serve with a white sauce (see recipe accompanying Asparagus With Cheese recipe on page 61).

1920 CHOU SHELLS

Now that you're an old expert at making Timbales, Chou Shells should be a cinch! "CHOU" means "cabbage" in French, which is an unlikely title for a dough. But when this marvelous dough rises it puffs up and looks somewhat like the curving surface of a cabbage. The terriffic thing about this pastry dough is that it can be transformed into a dessert pastry shell, or main course shell, or even a biscuit for soups (with just a slight change in the recipe). But let's make the basic dough for now. You'll need:

½ cup butter   1 cup sifted flour
1 cup boiling water   4 unbeaten eggs

Put the butter and water in a saucepan, and let them reach the boiling point. Add flour, and stir vigorously. (This should form a mess in the center of your pan.) Remove that pan from the fire, but keep on stirring for another 30 seconds or so. Set aside for three minutes.

Add your eggs, one at a time, to your flour mixture, stirring as you go. Now is the time you must decide what you are going to fill your shells with. If it is going to be an entrée you'll want to add a pinch of salt to dough. If it is to be a dessert, add 2 teaspoons of powdered sugar! And if you are going to make soup or salad puffs with nothing inside, stir in two tablespoons of finely grated cheese, and season with salt and paprika.

Have a pan or greased cookie sheet ready, and drop the chou paste by spoonfuls, or press through a pastry bag and tube. You can make these in different shapes. For example: if you had fish, you could make a long shell so that the whole fish could fit inside (especially nice when using those small little fish called Smeltz!). On the other hand, if you were stuffing your shells with something smaller, you could make cream-puff sized-shells. At any rate, make sure the mounds are well separated, and bake for half an hour. Bake at a higher heat (450°) for the first 10 minutes, and then reduce the heat to 350° for the rest of the time (about 20 to 25 minutes). To test for doneness, take out one of the puffs and let it stand for two or three minutes. If it doesn't fall, it's done.

When the shells are cool, split them and fill. You can, if you like, use the top half for one thing, and the bottom half for another. They can also be re-heated.

Use your imagination to stuff these shells. You can use scallops, oysters, crabmeat, and so on, with a rich newburg sauce. Fill them with fresh fruit, creamed corn, cheese, or, for a spectacular dessert, add some melted chocolate to your paste before baking, and fill the cooled puff with ice cream! If you want an even richer dessert, cover with chocolate sauce!

Try filling your shells with all kinds of puddings and pie fillings, and topping with meringue.

For an afternoon treat with tea, make thimble-sized shells and fill them with jam, marmalade, cream cheese, nuts, capers, chopped olives, and so on.

Salads

Salads

1930 CABBAGE, APPLE AND WALNUT SALAD

Rinso-white, Rinso-bright! Remember the cheery whistle? While the wash was going, perhaps some of the homemakers of the day were working up this tasty salad.

½ cup walnuts	⅛ teaspoon salt
1 cup chopped tart apples	Mayonnaise
1 cup shredded cabbage	Paprika

Break the walnuts into pieces, and then toss the apple pieces, nuts and cabbage together. Add salt and enough mayonnaise to coat the ingredients, no more. Serve on whole cabbage leaves and garnish, and top with a whole walnut, additional mayonnaise, and just a pinch of paprika for coloring.

1934 CHEESE PEANUT SALAD

Long before Jimmy Carter brought the peanut to our attention, a food economist somewhere in the city of New York came up with this hot weather treat. The year was 1934, and these were the ingredients:

½ cup cracker crumbs	1 cup shredded lettuce
½ cup chopped salted peanuts	½ cup chopped celery
1 cup cottage cheese	Salt
1½ cups chopped cabbage	Thousand Island Dressing

Combine your crumbs, peanuts, cheese, and vegetables. Season to your own taste. Add Thousand Island Dressing, and serve.

1931 SPRING RADISH SALAD

Spring brings a whole new world of fresh vegetables, and radishes are plentiful. Here's a salad that features them along with green onions (scallions).

Radishes   **Scallions (or green onions)**
Your favorite French dressing **Hearts of lettuce**

Slice the radishes in very thin slices (you can use a carrot peeler), and marinate them in the French dressing. Chop up just the white part of the scallions, and add that to the mixture. After the marinade has had time to take effect (about an hour) place this mixture on hearts of lettuce, and top with more French dressing.

FRESH WATERCRESS AND PIMIENTO SALAD

This recipe is from the early 30's.

Pimento   **Highly seasoned French**
Fresh watercress   **dressing**
Cheese cracker crumbs

You can use either pre-cut thin strips of pimento, or the whole pimentos cut into decorative shapes with small cutters. Mix this with fresh watercress and top with cheese cracker crumbs. You can make your own by using plain crackers topped with grated cheese that have been toasted slightly in your oven. When ready, crumble them, and use accordingly. Use a highly seasoned French dressing, and pour it over the salad.

STRAWBERRY AND CELERY SALAD
WITH HONEY DRESSING

This is an unusual combination that happens to taste terrific!

Fresh strawberries   **Celery**

Cut the strawberries in half, lengthwise, and set aside. Use half the amount of celery as strawberries, and measure by slicing the celery in thin, short strips. Now you'll want to make your "honey dressing."

Honey Dressing:

6 tablespoons olive oil   ¼ cup honey
1 tablespoon salt   ¼ teaspoon paprika
2 tablespoons lemon juice

Combine the olive oil, salt, lemon juice, honey, and paprika and beat until frothy. Drain the strawberries and add them along with the celery in a salad bowl. Serve with the Honey Dressing.

Here's a 1933 article that could save us energy today!

Turn on the Hot Water

THE use of all kinds of automatic water heaters is so prevalent that a reminder of some of the ways in which hot water can be of help in doing the housework may be timely.

CERTAIN fresh stains can be effectively removed from table linen by stretching it in embroidery loops and holding it under the running faucet. Coffee, tea and various fruits yield to hot water.

HOT water used for sprinkling clothes penetrates evenly and rapidly. A garment dampened with hot water and rolled tight will be ready for the iron or ironing machine within fifteen or twenty minutes. Bluing or dye for tinting should be dissolved in a small amount of warm water to avoid streaks or spots on the clean clothes.

TEPID or even warmer water removes grit, sand and dirt quickly from vegetables, especially spinach and broccoli, carrots, potatoes, celery, leaf lettuce and beets.

STARTING vegetables in boiling water shortens the time of cooking, decreases the loss of food value and helps them to keep their color.

FINGER marks may be washed off furniture with soapsuds. Never use too much water and be sure it is tepid or a little warmer, but be generous of soapy lather, keeping it dry. Follow this by wiping off with a cloth wrung from clear water, dry with a lintless cloth and then polish with your favorite furniture polish or liquid wax. For mahogany use one chamois for the washing and another for the rinsing and drying.

HOT water helps defrost the refrigerator when you haven't much time. Fill trays with it and set in position. Turn off the current. If you want ice quickly after defrosting, fill the trays with hot water turn on current and cubes will freeze with surprising speed.

MOLDED gelatine desserts and salads and foods frozen in the refrigerator trays may be removed in perfect condition for serving if you set their containers in a pan of hot water for a few seconds. Beware of leaving them there too long.

Rice,
Potatoes, Casseroles,
and Vegetables

Rice, Potatoes, Casseroles, and Vegetables

FRIED RICE

Here's a Chinese dish that comes from a turn-of-the-century magazine. Many of us across the United States are not fortunate enough to have access to some of the more exotic Chinese ingredients needed for many dishes, but this one calls for easily accessible things like rice, and vegetables.

4 bowls cooked rice
¼ pound chicken or pork,
  cut into cubes
2 cups vegetables (Chinese
  if available)

5 eggs
1 cup stock or soup

Put the rice in a hot oiled pan and cook it until it changes color. Make sure and turn it frequently; set aside. Now fry the chicken and vegetables for 3 minutes in a separate hot oiled pan (if you can get peanut oil so much the better). Add cold water and cook for 15 minutes. Pour off the water and add the rice. Beat the eggs well and add to the rice. Add the soup and continue to cook until the eggs appear to be done.

To Wring Hot Cloths
A new use for a potato ricer is as a substitute for the hands when wringing out hot cloths in case of illness. It not only enables one to use very hot water, but protects the hands. This is particularly true if hot applications must be continued for some time.

1918 NUT HASH

If you're a gardener you will appreciate this. In 1918 Burpee's Seeds would mail you one seed packet of Golden Bantam sweet corn, one of their earliest Black Red Ball Beets, another of Earliest Wayahead Lettuce, still another packet of Chalks early Jewel Tomato, and finally a packet of their improved Bush Lima Beans, for 25¢. They tell you in their ads that if you bought these separately, they would cost you 50¢. That's not a bad deal.

In 1918, Ivory Soap was trying to get magazine readers to purchase their soap and make a paste of it to clean leather and other materials which were not adaptable to suds. The recipe for the paste was printed on the inside wrapper of the soap.

This is something else that came along in 1918. Nut Hash. It's very good, has 1818 calories in all, and 216 of them are protein.

2 tablespoons bacon drippings
2 tablespoons minced onion
2 tablespoons peanut butter
1 cup milk
1 quart chopped cooked
   potatoes

1 cup chopped celery
1 cup broken nut meats
1 shredded green pepper
Salt and pepper to taste

Put the drippings in a frying pan. Add the minced onion, and fry until it is a deep yellow. Add your peanut butter and milk next, stirring constantly, until everything comes to a boil. Add the potatoes, celery, nut meats, and green pepper, and season them with the salt and pepper. Mix thoroughly. Cook for about half an hour over a low flame, and stir occasionally. Serve hot.

1931 POTATOES GALOSCHE

6 large potatoes
¼ cup butter, softened
1 teaspoon salt

¼ teaspoon white pepper
3 tablespoons chopped parsley
1 teaspoon grated lemon rind

Pare your potatoes and cut them in the shape of wooden shoes. If you don't feel up to being quite that artistic, make them into potato balls, or just their regular shape. I don't know about you, but when a recipe says to make wooden shoes, mine always come out looking like galoshes. Anyway . . . cook your potato shoes, balls, or whatever, in boiling salted water til tender; drain, and pour the following sauce over them. To make this sauce you'll need to cream the butter in a warm dish until it is very soft, add the seasonings, parsley and lemon rind, and serve. Use only the yellow part of the lemon rind . . . not the white!

1948 SOUR CREAM POTATO CASSEROLE

We go back to 1948 for this recipe. You'll need 40 minutes and the following ingredients:

2 tablespoons butter
⅔ cup chopped onion
3 cups sliced, cooked potatoes
Salt and pepper
½ cup bran cereal (crushed to
    fine crumbs)

4 tablespoons grated
    American cheese
1 cup sour cream
2 eggs, beaten
½ teaspoon salt
Dash of pepper

Melt the butter and cook the onion in it until it's tender. Place half of the potatoes in a buttered casserole dish and sprinkle them with salt and pepper. Add part of the onion, bran, and cheese. Mix the sour cream, eggs, salt, plus pepper. Pour this mixture over the potatoes. Repeat, with another layer of potatoes, cheese mixture, and sour cream mixture. Bake at 350° for 20 to 30 minutes.

MAKING CASSEROLES

Casserole is another of those French words that takes us three or four words to explain. It means "covered baking dish," and it is a great way to save time, dishes, and money. Time (because it goes from the oven to the table), dishes, (because you can serve it in today's great oven-to-table wear) and money (because you can use leftovers, less expensive cuts of meat, and other things you have handy in your refrigerator). A 1920 article on casseroles suggests that any easy casserole can be made just by adding your vegetables with a small amount of water or stock (chopping your vegetables up into bite-sized pieces), and seasoning with about ½ teaspoon of pepper and 1 tablespoon of salt to every cup of vegetables used. Vegetables they suggested for this dish or dishes are: asparagus, beans, beets, brussel sprouts, cabbage, cauliflower, kale, kohlrabi, onions, parsnips, peas, potatoes, rutabagas, spinach, squash, sweet corn, Swiss chard, tomatoes and turnips. Have they left anything out???

ROUND STEAK AND SWEET POTATO CASSEROLE

You can make a round steak casserole by cutting leftover cooked steak into bite-sized pieces and adding it to your casserole. Or, add medium-sized sweet potatoes that have been cut in halves lengthwise, and parboiled until they are soft. Then melt 3 tablespoons of butter in your casserole dish, and add the sweet potatoes, sprinkled with ground cinnamon, and brown sugar; cover. Bake at 350° until hot and done. You can add all kinds of vegetables to this or use just the potatoes.

1919 GREEN ONIONS WITH DRAWN BUTTER

When I was a girl, we called green onions "scallions" . . . and I can remember my mother using them as a bit of color to garnish a salad more than as a vegetable. Until this recipe, I had never heard of boiling them . . . and the results are too good to be forgotten. You'll need:

One bunch of green onions	**A dash of salt**
with crisp tops	**Water to boil**

Wash your little green onions thoroughly, and trim off those stringy roots. Now trim the tops to a uniform length of 6 inches. Tie the onions in small bunches and cook in a large quantity of boiling water to which you have added a pinch of salt. Do not cover. When the onions are tender, drain the onions, untie the strings, and serve with the following:

Drawn Butter:

⅓ cup butter, divided	**½ teaspoon salt**
3 tablespoons flour	**Dash of pepper**

Melt half the butter over low heat; add the flour with the seasonings, and stir until smooth. Now add the hot water gradually, stirring constantly, and cook for 5 minutes. Now add the remaining half of butter, and serve.

1945 DEVILED BEETS

2 cups sliced, cooked beets
3 tablespoons butter
2 tablespoons prepared
  mustard
2 tablespoons honey

1 teaspoon Worcestershire
  sauce
½ teaspoon salt
¼ teaspoon paprika

Place the beets in a shallow casserole dish. Melt the butter in a saucepan, and add the mustard, honey, and Worcestershire sauce. Season with salt and paprika, and heat well. Pour the sauce over the beets in the casserole dish and bake at 350° for 15 minutes.

LIMA BEAN MEDLEY

Here's another of those reader recipes, which often times are better than the ones the magazines' economists work up. You'll need:

2 cups diced celery
1 small onion, chopped
1 bell pepper, chopped
2 tablespoons vegetable oil or
  other cooking fat
2 cups boiling water

2 fresh or canned tomatoes,
  quartered
2 cups canned or cooked lima
  beans
Salt and pepper
½ (3 oz.) package egg noodles

Cook the celery and onion along with the bell pepper in fat til brown. Now add water and simmer til almost done. Add your tomatoes and lima beans, salt and pepper. Keep simmering til done, adding more water, if necessary. Boil your noodles according to package directions, and add them to the vegetables. Makes 8 servings.

1921 ASPARAGUS WITH CHEESE

If you are a lot like me, there are some vegetables you refused to even try as a child, that you love as an adult. Asparagus is one of "those" vegetables for me . . . along with brussel sprouts, and cabbage. Here's an especially tempting asparagus recipe that may even get some of the youngsters enthused.

2 pounds fresh asparagus
2 tablespoons butter
2 tablespoons flour
¼ teaspoon salt

1 cup asparagus stock
½ cup milk
¼ cup grated cheese

Wash the asparagus, trimming off the coarse parts; tie them in bunches. Cook asparagus in a deep kettle, in boiling salted water. Use as a rule of thumb one teaspoon of salt for one quart of water. Stand the asparagus up so that the tips are out of water. Partially cover the kettle, and boil until the lower part of the asparagus is tender.

Now make a white sauce by melting the butter in a saucepan; add flour and salt, stirring constantly, until smooth. Add the asparagus stock gradually, and stir after each addition. Add the milk, stirring constantly, and cook for 5 minutes. Place the asparagus in a greased pan and pour your sauce over it, sprinkling cheese on the top. Bake in a moderate oven (375°) til the cheese melts and browns.

1928 CREAMED MUSHROOMS

You'll give away your age if you remember the Motor Coat, and tuck-away turbon. They were popular in 1928, the same year that this recipe came out. Have ready:

1 pound fresh mushrooms or
   1 large can chopped
   mushrooms, drained
3 tablespoons butter
4 tablespoons butter
4 tablespoons flour
2½ cups chicken stock or
   milk
1 egg, slightly beaten

1 teaspoon Worcestershire
   sauce
½ teaspoon salt
½ teaspoon paprika
Strips of green pepper
Strips of pimento
Parsley
Stuffed olives

Peel and slice your fresh mushrooms and sauté them in 3 table-spoons butter for about 10 minutes. (If you are using canned mush-rooms be sure and drain them first). Make the white sauce by melting 4 tablespoons butter in a saucepan and stirring in the flour, blending well. Add the stock or milk, stirring constantly. Cook until smooth. Stir constantly to prevent lumps. Place the mixture in a double-boiler over hot water; add a slightly beaten egg, stirring constantly until blended. Stir in Worcestershire sauce, salt, paprika, and mushrooms. Don't add the green peppers or pimento until just before you serve the dish. Garnish with parsley and stuffed olives. Serve, if you wish, upon hot toast cut into triangles.

1944 GREEN TOMATO PIE

Here's a recipe from 1944. It was an election year. The creator of Peter Rabbit, Beattrix Potter, was dead at 77. Jimmy Durante was on CBS for Camel cigarettes, and Little LuLu was the spokeswoman for Kleenex. On the "homefront," women were trying to cope with the meat shortage with recipes like this one. You'll need:

Pastry for a double-crust
   9-inch pie
½ cup sugar
2 tablespoons flour
Grated rind of 1 lemon
¼ teaspoon ground allspice

¼ teaspoon salt
4 cups peeled and sliced green
   tomatoes
1 tablespoon lemon juice
3 tablespoons butter

Line a pie pan with pie dough or use a ready-made crust. Mix the sugar, flour, lemon rind, allspice, and salt together. Sprinkle just a little of this at the bottom of the pie shell. Arrange the tomato slices, a layer at a time, as you cover each layer with the sugar mixture, lemon juice, and a dot of butter on each slice. Keep layering until you reach the top of the pie tin. Cover with a latticed top and bake at 350° for 45 minutes.

1943 BAKED BEAN SANDWICH

This one was a new one on me. Baked beans . . . in a sandwich? Yes, said a smart reader in Columbus, Ohio, and she gave these ingredients to prove it:

1 cup baked beans
¼ cup chopped walnuts
¼ cup chopped celery
2 tablespoons minced onion

¼ teaspoon salt
1 tablespoon chopped pickle
2 tablespoons ketchup
Buttered whole wheat bread

Now just combine everything, except bread, and mix well. Spread on buttered whole wheat bread. Makes about 1½ cups.

1918 CURRIED RADISHES

Radishes are kind of step-vegetables . . . You don't see too much attention paid to them in modern cookbooks. We offer this second recipe for a special flavor . . . and in honor of, the radish.

Choose one packet or bunch of young tender round radishes   **Boiling salted water**

Remove the tops and roots of your radishes and put the vegetables in cold water to crisp. Drain from the cold water, and put them in a kettle with a large quantity of salted water. Figure on one teaspoon of salt for every quart of water. Cook rapidly, without a cover, until the radishes are nice and tender. Place them in a vegetable dish; for every two cups of radishes pour over one cup of the curry sauce:

Curry Sauce:

2 tablespoons butter
2 tablespoons flour
½ teaspoon salt

½ teaspoon curry powder
⅛ teaspoon pepper
1 cup milk

Melt your butter in a saucepan; add the flour, and seasonings, and stir until well blended. Now add your milk gradually, stirring constantly, and let the sauce boil between each addition. Pour sauce over radishes, and serve!

1941 CABBAGE STUFFED WITH APPLES

In 1941 people were careful about what they used in Industry and elsewhere. In order to save steel for defense, we relied on stainless steel, which used less of the precious commodity. Even our new stream-lined trains were made of it. It was a time of Gable, Lamarr, and Robert Young—a time for cabbage, stuffed with apples. You'll need:

1 medium-sized head cabbage	3 medium-to-large apples
2 cups hot water	¼ cup firmly packed brown
1 teaspoon salt	sugar
3 strips bacon, minced and	3 tablespoons vinegar
cooked	Salt and pepper to taste
½ teaspoon pepper	2 tablespoons butter

Shred the cabbage, and put it in a lightly greased casserole dish. Add the hot water, 1 teaspoon salt, bacon, ½ teaspoon pepper, and mix them all together. Cover and bake at 375° for 20 minutes. Pare and core the apples. Remove the casserole from the oven, make indentations in cabbage mixture; place the apples in the holes. Fill the very center of the apples with brown sugar and vinegar, and sprinkle lightly with salt and pepper. Dot with butter, and cover. Return the casserole to the 375° oven for another 30 minutes, and serve. Enough to feed 4 or even 6.

1927 VIRGINIA OKRA STEW

This 1927 recipe comes from a readers recipe column. She calls for ½ shin of beef. Let your butcher translate for you.

1 gallon water
½ shin of beef
1 quart fresh tomatoes, cut
　　into pieces
4 small onions, thinly sliced
2 green sweet peppers, thinly
　　sliced

1 pint fresh okra, thinly sliced
½ yellow turnip, diced
Seasonings as desired
Boiled rice

Pour a gallon of water into a big pot; add beef and simmer until the liquid is reduced in half. Add the tomatoes, onions, and green peppers. Now add okra. Cover, and cook slowly until the mixture becomes nice and thick. This should take about 4 hours. Season to your taste; serve hot with boiled rice. You might add a slice of lemon as a garnish, if desired. The total time in cooking this is about 7 hours, and makes 8 servings.

An Improved Washer

Addicts to basin washing will find it convenient to use a wire potato masher to force the fabrics up and down through the suds. It makes a little washing machine all complete, and eliminates the danger of rubbing or twisting delicate materials.

1932 RAISIN KIDNEY BEANS

It was Christmas, 1932. A lot of people were hungry for inexpensive meals that tasted good. This was one answer to their prayers.

1 cup raisins
½ cup diced bacon
½ cup chopped onion
2 cups canned vegetable soup
2 cups canned red kidney
  beans

½ cup liquid from beans
Tabasco sauce
Salt

Run water over the raisins and wash. Now drain and set aside. Fry the bacon until it's crisp; remove bacon and leave the pan on the stove. Add onion; fry onion until it's light brown in color. Now replace the bacon and raisins in the pan; fry until the raisins are plump. Then add the condensed soup and liquid from the beans to the raisin mixture; bring to a boil, and cook for two minutes. Now add the beans and Tabasco sauce. Season to taste. Mix well. Pour into a baking dish and bake at 375° for 40 minutes.

1942 DRYING VEGETABLES

If you're a catalog nut, like I am, you've seen some modern-day refinements of this recipe. They are now selling drying kits, which cost upwards of $45.00. With this recipe all you need is the sunshine, or a cool oven. It doesn't have any real set ingredients, and the recipe itself is more of a "how to" sort of affair.

Select really fresh vegetables for drying. Steam them by putting them in a colander and then putting the colander in a kettle with an inch of boiling water inside. Test the center of the vegetables to make sure they are heated throughout. When they are well heated, remove them from the steamer, and arrange them in trays about a half-inch deep, or less. Cookie trays do well. Racks will also do. Put these in a cool oven of 140°, or, on a bright summer day, dry them in the sun. Be sure and cover your vegetables with a piece of cheesecloth. When they are absolutely BONE DRY (whatever "bone dry" is), they can be stored. Test them by seeing if they will crumble. Store them in a cool, dry place. Shelled peas and string beans are good vegetables for drying. Just cut your beans in 1-inch lengths first. If you steam fresh spinach until it's wilted it will do nicely too. Don't forget sweet corn. Steam the corn—on the cob, until the milk is set, and then cut from the cob, and dry.

To eat your dried vegetables, soak them for 1 to 3 hours, using 6 to 8 times as much water as vegetables (less for corn); then cook them in the same water til done.

Cheesy Concoctions

Cheesy Concoctions

1916 CHEESE WAFERS

In 1916 fashion came out with a new material—Brittania. It had a new texture with the body of taffeta, and less luster than satin. Hats were "in." The economy-minded lady could get away with (we're told) two hats, an afternoon dress, a few correct blouses, and a one-piece dress of silk and chiffon cloth, together with such things as gloves, shoes, and so on. Some dresses seen in America's magazines were made of a gauze-like material called embroidered batiste, *with cobweb lace, along with fish net mesh. Mentioned too, are the high corsage and apron. Being a non-sewer, I am at a loss as to what a peplum is, or was, but many of the years' dresses had ripples of lace. Dresses were called "frocks." Hats were made of tiny dull black paillettes, and ornamented with a spray of black goura attached to the crown with a bunch of black ostrich feathers. This was the same year that this tasty quick recipe for Cheese Wafers came out.*

Chopped cheese or shredded cheese of your choice
Chopped green or black olives
A dash of cayenne pepper
Buttered toast or crackers
Halved walnut meats

Mix the cheese and chopped olives together. Add a dash of cayenne, and spread over buttered toast or crackers. Place in the oven under a low flame just long enough for the cheese to melt. Top with a walnut half, and serve hot. This makes a nice appetizer!

CHEESY CONCOCTIONS

1923 RINKTUM DIDDY

I love the name of this cheesy mixture. To make it you'll need:

One small onion, chopped
1 tablespoon melted butter
1 large can of tomatoes,
   strained
One pound of your favorite
   cheese, cut into small pieces

Paprika
Tabasco sauce
Worcestershire Sauce
Salt to taste
Two slightly beaten eggs
Saltine crackers

Fry your chopped onion in butter until tender. Add the tomatoes; heat to boiling, then add the cheese, stirring until the cheese melts. Add everything else but the eggs and saltines. Stir some of hot mixture into beaten eggs until well blended. Add egg mixture to remaining hot mixture, stirring constantly. Cook for 2 minutes on low heat, stirring constantly, until thickened. Serve with saltines.

To Use Up Tiny Potatoes

We had so many small potatoes this year, and as I have found an excellent way to use them, I want to pass it on. I boil them in salted water with the skins on and then run them through the potato ricer. The skins do not go through and the flavor is improved by the process. Then I usually put them in a baking dish, dot with butter and pepper, and brown in a hot oven. In this manner I have utilized over a bushel of potatoes that were too small to peel and would have been wasted otherwise.

Fish and Chicken

Fish and Chicken

THE $100 WINNER CREAMED LOBSTER

This 1922 recipe won a $100 prize for a lucky New Yorker. It's not as inexpensive as it once was, and it takes a good many ingredients, but it is delicious! You'll need:

3 tablespoons of butter or margarine (while you're spending all of this money on lobster you might as well splurge and use real butter)

1 cup mushrooms, broken in pieces (canned will do just fine)

½ small onion, sliced

1 tablespoon minced green pepper

1 tablespoon minced parsley (fresh is better)

1 tablespoon pimento, cut into small pieces

2 tablespoons flour

½ teaspoon salt

Dash of cayenne pepper

2 cups diced boiled lobster

1¾ cups evaporated milk

¾ cup water

2 beaten egg yolks

These older recipes often call for a double boiler. These days a heavy enameled pot will do just as well, or if you can find a mock element in your hardware store use it. It looks like a round flat piece of stainless with holes in it, and it has a handle. I'm sure it has a technical name of sorts, but if you ask the salesman he or she will know what you're talking about. These wonderful inventions cost less than $2, and do the same job as a double boiler. Anyway—back to the recipe.

Melt your butter in your pan or double boiler; add the vegetables and cook, while stirring, for about 10 minutes. Now add your flour, and spices; mix well. Combine your milk and water and save half a cup for a later time. Add the remaining two cups milk mixture to the flour mixture (slowly). Now add your lobster, and cook for another 10 minutes. Just before dinner combine remaining half-cup of milk and water you put aside with the egg yolks; pour it into the lobster mixture. Cook for about five minutes and serve.

1947 SOLE AUX CHAMPIGNONS

In 1947 Katherine Hepburn and Paul Hendreid starred in "Song of Love" for MGM, companies were coming out with post-war products to lure anxious consumers, women all over the country were buying themselves a basic black dress. Incidentally, those "basic blacks" were mid-calf length. Our fashion pages were filled with hats and—veils— remember them? They gave a woman an air of mystery! As it was hard to eat with a veil turned over one's face, I'm sure the ladies took off their hats to this dish. You'll need:

3 pounds fillet of sole
Melted butter or margarine
Salt
Black pepper
Paprika
Melted butter or margarine
1½ pounds fresh mushrooms
Salt
5 tablespoons flour
6 tablespoons melted butter
¼ to ⅓ cup sherry
Milk to taste

Sauce left over from sautéing
    mushrooms
1 tablespoon grated onion
1 teaspoon sweet basil leaves
1 teaspoon chopped fresh or
    dried parsley
⅛ teaspoon cayenne pepper
½ pound grated Parmesan
    cheese
1 pound cooked and peeled
    fresh shrimp
Dash of Tabasco

Wash your fillets and pat them dry. Sauté them in hot butter for about a minute on each side, and then put them in a shallow baking pan. Sprinkle with salt, pepper, and paprika. Set aside. Now take those mushrooms and choose the 12 or 14 with the best caps. Slice up the rest of the mushrooms and sauté them in butter for just a few minutes—just long enough to remove some of the moisture. Salt, and drain mushrooms, but remember to save the liquid. Spread the sautéed mushrooms over the sole. Now you are going to make a sauce with that leftover butter from sautéing the mushrooms. Add to it 6 tablespoons of butter, flour, and about 1 cup of milk. I say "about" because it will depend on how much of that mushroom liquid you have left, and your choice of amounts of sherry. All in all, when everything is added together, you should have about 2 cups of liquid. Add the onion, sweet basil, parsley, and cayenne pepper. Put the mixture in either a double boiler, or a heavy saucepan, and add the grated Parmesan cheese. Now add your cooked shrimp. To make bite-sized portions, you might consider halving the shrimp before adding them to the mixture. (The look of whole shrimp is prettier.) Cook just long enough to melt the cheese and add a little salt and a dash of tabasco for flavor. Spoon the sauce over the mushrooms and sole, and sprinkle the whole thing with a little more cheese and paprika. If you have any remaining shrimp, border the dish with them, followed by an inside border of those nice caps you'd been saving. If not, just use the caps (stem-side down, of course). Dot everything with butter; bake at 350° for 30 minutes. When finished, run under the broiler for a moment so as to make a crusty top.

1920 FILLET OF BASS WITH GRAPE SAUCE

8 fillets of bass	2 cups cold water
½ teaspoon salt	¼ teaspoon salt
Juice of one lemon	2 tablespoons butter
3 sliced carrots	3 tablespoons flour
1 slice of onion	1 cup skinned and seeded
1 piece bay leaf	white grapes

Place the fillets on a plate; sprinkle them with salt. Pour lemon juice on top of them. Wrap the fish in cheesecloth and steam for 15 minutes. Now remove the fish to a serving dish and pour the grape sauce around them. To make the sauce, put the skin and bones of the fish with the carrots, onion, and bay leaf in salted cold water, in a saucepan. Cook to the boiling point; cook slowly for about half an hour. Rub cooked mixture through a strainer back into saucepan. Thicken with butter and flour. Cream together the entire sauce mixture; add the grapes. Cook one more minute and pour sauce over the fish.

1943 FISH FILLETS WITH WINE SAUCE

In 1943 everyone was conscious of what they could do to help out fighting men overseas. Women were digging up their old silk stocking and contributing them to the cause: 15 pair made one powder bag for the military. Kool-aid was still 5¢, Johnny was out there calling for Phillip Morris, and women were experimenting with new home permanents. "For the duration" became part of the language, and this recipe was part of a group selected by one 1943 magazine to help the housewife cook good, meatless meals.

2 tablespoons minced onion	½ cup Sauterne wine
1 tablespoon oil	1 pound fresh or quick frozen
2 tablespoons flour	cod or haddock fillets
1½ teaspoons salt	1 tablespoon chopped fresh
⅛ teaspoon pepper	parsley
½ cup cream (top milk)	

Sauté the onion in the hot oil in a heavy enameled pan, or double boiler until tender. Stir in the flour, salt, and pepper, blending well. Add milk, stirring constantly and cook until thickened. When thickened remove, and very gradually stir in the wine. Put the fish in a baking pan, and sprinkle with salt. Pour the sauce over fish. Bake at 350° for half an hour, basting often. Sprinkle with parsley and serve. Serves 4.

1935 FISH HASH

In 1935 you could turn your radio on and hear "Jello again, this is Jack Benny!" Believe it or not, you could feed a family of 10 on $18 a week, and buy a tin of aspirin for 15¢. You could also make this tempting fish recipe with cold, flaked fish.

2 cups cold, flaked fish
1 cup chopped boiled potato
3 slices crisp bacon, diced
Salt
1 teaspoon chopped fresh
   parsley

1 tablespoon chopped onion
½ teaspoon dried thyme
Pepper

Mix everything together well, and cook slowly in a well-buttered hot pan until it becomes crispy and brown. Serve with ketchup, and cole slaw for lunch, or with a broiled tomato slice for breakfast.

That Cloudy Effect on Furniture

When highly polished furniture acquires a cloudy tinge, wipe it with a cloth wrung tightly out of warm water to which one table-spoonful of vinegar has been added and polish with a soft dry cloth.

1945 SALMON AND CHEESE CASSEROLE

The year was 1945. Women were adorning the country's beaches with skirted bathing suits, and Frank and Nancy Sinatra had a son, Frances Wayne. Magazine home economists all over America were trying to come up with taste-tempting dishes that didn't cost a whole heck of a lot. This was one of them.

1½ cups scalded milk
1 cup soft bread crumbs
1 tablespoon minced parsley
1½ tablespoons minced onion
1½ cups grated processed
  cheese (American or
  Cheddar)
⅜ teaspoon salt
⅛ teaspoon pepper

A dash of paprika
3 eggs (beaten til foamy)
1 cup leftover cooked
  vegetables (fresh or canned)
1 cup cooked flaked fresh or
  canned salmon (or other
  similar fish)
Warm water

Pour the milk over the bread crumbs in a bowl; add the parsley, onion, and cheese. Now add the seasonings and add your eggs. Pour the whole mixture over the vegetables and fish which have been arranged in the bottom of a 1½-quart casserole dish. Set the casserole dish in a baking pan or broiler tray filled with about an inch of warm water. Bake at 325° for 75 minutes or until firm. Serves 6.

1941 BUB'S CHICKEN

Back in 1941 gasoline companies sold more than gasoline and oil. They sold rest rooms and cleanliness. Magazine ads featured a mother and daughter freshening up by a mirror in a sparkling rest room. Other ads featured service-station men in uniform—with caps and bow ties completing the outfit. It was a time when you could buy a whole chicken, with feet included. When you made chicken soup, you used the feet to give flavor and strength to the soup. These days health laws forbid such sales and women rely on bones to give body to their chicken soup. This recipe lets you cook your chicken in soup if you like. It's one of my favorites.

Water to cover	Pickling spices
1 chicken, cut up	Salt, pepper, and garlic salt
Bay leaf	Paprika
4 chicken bouillon cubes	1 onion, sliced (for fat)
2 carrots	Chicken fat, melted (about
2 stalks celery	12 ounces)
2 onions	Ketchup

In order to make this 1941 recipe, you must first render your chicken fat by cooking it in a pot with a sliced onion and a dash of salt. When it's melted, pour it through a sieve and chill until ready to use. Next, place chicken in a large kettle, cover with water, and add vegetables, salt and pepper, and bouillon cubes. When the stock is done and the chicken is one step away from falling off the bones, take the chicken out of the stock and put the pieces into a baking pan. Brush with chicken fat. Sprinkle chicken with salt, pepper, garlic salt and a handful of pickling spices. Sprinkle with paprika. Bake at 350° for 20 minutes; turn, and coat in the same manner with fat and paprika. Bake another 20 minutes. Mix half cup each ketchup and fat, and brush top of chicken. Bake another 10 to 15 minutes, basting every so often. Chicken is done when the ketchup has "baked on" look. Don't brush on ketchup mixture too thickly. Use stock as soup, adding a teaspoon of dill seeds for flavor. Serve soup with wide noodles.

1916 CHICKEN TRUFFLES

There were all kinds of new-fangled inventions being tested in 1916. A domestic experiment station was set up in the east, where housewives tested electric coffee grinders, fireless cookers, electric hotplates, stoves, and dishwashers (called "washing machines for dishes," cleverly enough). There were ice boxes, incinerators, and smokeless oil heaters in this laboratory. In the real world, soup cost 10¢ a can and you were making a living wage at $4 a day. This recipe comes from that same year, and calls for the following:

1 can of mushrooms, chopped or about half a pint, if fresh	1 teaspoon flour
Water	1 tablespoon butter
1 pound cooked chicken, finely chopped	Seasonings, as desired
	Toast

Cover the mushrooms with water, and boil for 5 minutes. Skim out the mushrooms into a hot dish, and you should have about a cup of liquid left in the pan. Thicken this with a teaspoon of flour, a tablespoon of butter, and season well. Add the chicken and mushrooms; heat, and stir well. Serve on small pieces of toast.

1943 CURRIED CHICKEN FRICASSÉE

This 1943 recipe came at a time when WPB restrictions gave us a choice of only 3 kinds of umbrellas (the least of our problems), "fooling around" and "swishy" had entirely modest meanings, and Veronica Lake was starring in "Star Spangled Rhythm" for Paramount. A leading womans' magazine offered this 1943 recipe, along with a suggestion that you serve it with brown rice, cabbage, and raw carrot sticks.

10 tablespoons flour
2½ teaspoons salt, divided
⅛ teaspoon pepper
1 (3½ pound) chicken,
  cut up
6 tablespoons oil or fat

6 tablespoons flour
1¼ teaspoons curry powder
1½ cups milk
1½ cups hot water
½ pound peeled, small white
  onions

Combine 10 tablespoons flour with ½ teaspoon of salt and ⅛ teaspoon pepper; roll the chicken pieces in this mixture. Sauté chicken in heated fat in a covered skillet until browned. Remove chicken. Now stir in 6 tablespoons of flour, remaining 2 teaspoons salt, and ½ teaspoon curry powder, blending well. Stir in the milk and water, cooking til thickened. Place the chicken pieces back in the skillet along with the onions; cover, and simmer til tender (about 2½ hours). When ready to serve, skim off the surface fat and add ¾ teaspoon of curry powder. Serves four.

POULET DE JOUR DE L'AN

In case you are wondering, all of that French means "New Year's Chicken."

1 chicken, cut in pieces	½ cup of cooking sherry or
2 carrots, diced	white grape juice
8 small boiling onions, peeled	1 dozen to 1¼ dozen
1 turnip, diced	mushrooms, chopped
1 clove of garlic, chopped	Flour

To make this 1931 recipe, place the pieces of chicken in a large pot and simmer over a low flame along with your carrots, onions, diced turnip, garlic clove (make sure this is chopped *very* fine). Add sherry or juice. Turn the chicken from time to time with care, basting with your vegetable and wine liquid. But for the most part keep the lid on the pot so that you steam cook your chicken. Cook for about 1 hour, depending on how low your flame is. During the last half hour, add the mushrooms. Serve with the vegetable sauce thickened by a little flour.

Note: You might want to add a little bit of butter and brown sugar for added flavor.

1945 CHICKEN IN SOUR CREAM

Everyone loved the movies in the mid 40's and why not! Beautiful screen stars like Anne Baxter touted all sorts of home and personal products ("nine out of ten screen stars use it"), and the public loved it. Just like they did this delicious chicken dinner. It becomes something really special when arranged over rice or buttered noodles.

½ cup minced onion
¼ cup hot fat
1 large frying chicken (2½ to
  3½ pounds), cut up
1 teaspoon paprika
1 teaspoon salt

2 tablespoons hot water
1 cup sour cream
1 tablespoon flour
1½ tablespoons cold water
¼ teaspoon lemon juice

Sauté onion in fat until tender. Remove onion. Brown the chicken pieces in the remaining fat. Add the onion again, plus the paprika, salt, and hot water. Cover and simmer over a low heat for about 30 minutes (or until tender). Take out the chicken and stir in the sour cream. Blend flour with cold water. When heated, add flour and water mixture and blend. Cook until it is nice and smooth and thick, stir in the lemon juice, and put the chicken back in the pan. Heat through. Serves 4.

1918 SALMI OF CHICKEN

Across the country, people were saving wheat by using substitutes. Every 1¾ pounds of bread manufactured by bakers under the Food Administration Regulations was equal to one pound of wheat flour. Women of 1918 were wearing coat dresses, ostrich plumes, and dark colors like maroon and navy. Advertisements in America's magazines urged the consumer to wash their hair with tar soap, use yeast foam, and use substitute wheat cake flour (with less sugar) made from rice. This recipe called for bread crumbs, and I wonder what it tasted like at that time, using this strange system of substitutions. You'll need:

Bread crumbs   **Sage**
Minced cooked chicken **Butter**
Salt   **Lemon juice**
Pepper   **Butter pats**
Celery salt   **Tomato sauce**

Cover the bottom of a baking dish with bread crumbs; add a layer of chicken. Season, and dot with butter and lemon juice. Add another layer of bread crumbs and so on until you get to the top of the pan. Top with pats of butter. Cover, and bake in a 9-inch square baking pan for 35 minutes at 325°. Take the top off at the last 10 minutes to brown. Serve with tomato sauce.

Meats

Meats

1932 LOUISIANA PUT-TOGETHER

1932—remember? Those were the days of Frank Parker (the gypsy tenor) long before he met up with Arthur Godfrey. Countess Olga Albani was a concert soprano, and Mildred Bailey was singing up a storm with Paul Whiteman's Orchestra. In the kitchen, paper towels on a roll were introduced for the first time. It's interesting to read a for-the-first-time description of how these towels were perforated so that the individual towels could be torn off easily. This 1932 recipe doesn't need any special meat, although flank steak does nicely. You can use your leftover roast and vegetables.

¾ pound beef	1½ teaspoons salt
4 tablespoons melted shortening	⅛ teaspoon pepper
3 onions, sliced	1 cup leftover cooked vegetables
1 green pepper, sliced	8 stuffed olives, sliced
1 cup tomato soup	1 cup rice, steamed
1 cup diced celery	

Cut your meat into very thin slices, and then fry in a hot skillet filled with melted shortening until brown and crisp. Remove the meat, and set aside. Now cook the onions and green pepper in the shortening until they are soft. Add the tomato soup, meat, celery, and seasonings and simmer until the onions and celery are tender. Add your leftover vegetables (things like peas, string beans, and carrots), and olives. This should be served on top of the steamed rice. Parsley makes a nice garnish.

1923 STEAK AND PURE CREAM

I use Rib-eyes, but you can also use Sirloins or T-Bones for this easy-to-fix dinner. Save it for company, or a special treat. It's super!

Rib-eye, Sirloin, or T-Bone steak (1½ inch thick)	Worcestershire sauce
Olive oil	1 pound fresh mushrooms
Salt, pepper to taste	2 tablespoons butter
	½ cup half-and-half

You'll want to marinate the steak in several tablespoons of olive oil which has been seasoned with salt, pepper, and Worcestershire sauce for at least three hours. Sear the meat on one side and then the other side. Then broil. Cook your mushrooms in butter which has been seasoned with salt and pepper. Make sure to stir the mushrooms often; add the cream to mushroom mixture, stirring well. When your steak is cooked to your liking put it on a serving platter and cover with mushrooms and cream.

1934 SPANISH MEATLOAF

I suppose meat loaf is one of my very favorite things to eat. You can do so many things with a pound or two of ground beef. Here's an interesting variation that made its way to many an oil-clothed kitchen table. The kids of the day might have said it was "Keen-O."

1 onion, chopped	2 cups cooked rice
1 clove garlic, chopped	12 small pimento-stuffed
2 tablespoons olive oil	olives
2 pounds lean pork, chopped	1 cup tomato pulp
1 beaten egg	

Put the onion and garlic in a pan that is hot with your oil. Add onion mixture to the meat, egg, rice, tomato pulp and olives; mix with a chopper. Pack mixture tightly into a loaf pan which has been greased. Bake at 350° for an hour and a half.

1920 AMERICAN GOULASH

This is a quick and easy recipe that will feed eight hungry people.

3 slices of bacon (make 'em
  nice and fatty)
1 large onion, sliced
1 pound hamburger
1 can red kidney beans
1 quart tomatoes

A pinch of salt
Pinch of cayenne pepper
Regular pepper
Sliced carrots
Cooked rice

Cut the bacon into small pieces and fry until crisp. Now add the onion and hamburger meat. Cook until the onion is golden and the meat is brown. Add the beans and tomatoes; cook for 15 minutes. You can now add the carrots or rice, or both, for variety.

1933 BAKED STEAK

In 1933 women were still using loose face powder regularly, and swearing by Listerine as a scalp conditioner. This recipe was published in a 1933 womens' magazine, and calls for the following:

Your favorite cut of steak, cut
  into pieces which have been
  slashed several times on
  each side (enough for two)
Flour
Hot fat
Salt and pepper for seasoning

Butter or margarine for
  greasing
1 onion, sliced
Celery leaves, or cut up pieces
  of celery
Ketchup
Boiling water

Flour your pieces of steak well, and sear in the hot fat until browned. Season with salt and pepper. Now butter a casserole dish, and line it with a layer of onion slices, celery or leaves, followed by the steak. Sprinkle with ketchup. Continue to layer with remaining ingredients, depending on how much steak you have, adding ketchup with each layer. Now cover with boiling water, and bake at 375° in a covered casserole dish for two hours.

1895 BEEF STEAK ROLLS

This is one of the oldest recipes in my collection. It leaves room for experimenting in that the food editor provided no particular stuffing recipe. So use your own favorite, and follow the simple directions below. You will need, besides your stuffing, the following:

A round steak (flank steak also does well)	Pepper
Your favorite stuffing	2 teaspoons butter
Salt	1 well-beaten egg
	Water

Pound the steak lightly, and spread the stuffing over it. Salt and pepper to taste, and add a little butter if you like. Lap over the ends and roll the steak up tightly. Tie closely with string or thread. Spread 2 teaspoons of butter over the rolled-up steak, and "wash" it with a well-beaten egg. Put some water in a small broiler pan with a rack over it, and put the beef rolls on top of the rack. Bake as you would duck or turkey, basting often. This takes 2½ hours at 300°. Serve with brown gravy. Remember to remove the string or thread before serving.

If you don't have a favorite stuffing recipe, use this one:

Stuffing:

2 chopped onions	1 teaspoon chopped parsley
¾ teaspoon salt	1 teaspoon crumbled dried
⅛ teaspoon pepper	sage or thyme leaves
Hot fat	1½ cups dried bread crumbs

Sauté the onions and seasonings in hot fat for about 2 or 3 minutes. Add the parsley and bread crumbs, and mix well. Spread this on the steak.

1947 BROWN BEEF BALLS IN ONION GRAVY

Remember Arthur Murray and his dance party? Well, in 1947, his "Girls" were on the pages of America's leading magazines promoting, of all things, deodorant. Tumble dryers were new on the market, as were flatplate and rotary ironers for the home. Leading appliance companies boasted automatic washers that could soak, wash, rinse, damp dry, clean themselves, and turn off automatically! Imagine. Here's a 1947 recipe that is just perfect for two people.

1½ cups sliced onions	¼ cup milk
3 tablespoons fat	2 tablespoons flour
½ pound ground beef	1½ cups water
2 tablespoons rolled oats	½ teaspoon Worcestershire
½ teaspoon salt	Sauce
⅛ teaspoon pepper	1 teaspoon meat extract (if
2 teaspoons minced onion	you can ever find such a
¾ teaspoon celery salt	thing)

First, sauté your onions until they are nice and tender in the fat; when the onions are done, remove them, but don't throw the fat away. Combine the next seven ingredients, mixing well. Drop meat mixture by tablespoons into the hot fat; brown on all sides, and remove to drain. Now, stir your flour into the fat, and brown as you stir. Add water, stirring constantly until it is blended. Add the rest of the ingredients, and return the meat and onions to the gravy. Cover, and simmer for 15 minutes.

1938 KIDNEY PIE

In 1938 an enterprising young Home Economist presented her readers with a group of recipes using less popular types and cuts of meat. This was among them.

1 veal kidney
1 beef bouillon cube
1 cup boiling water
2 tablespoons flour
¼ cup cold water

1 cup cubed potatoes, cooked
½ cup sliced carrots, cooked
1 small onion, chopped
Salt and pepper

First wash the kidney well. Cover with cold water and let stand for about an hour. Drain. Remove the cords and all of the center fat. Cut into small pieces. Now combine the bouillon cube and boiling water. Add the chopped kidney. Simmer for 20 minutes. Combine the flour and cold water, mixing well; add to the kidney mixture, stirring constantly until thickened and smooth. Add the cooked vegetables, and season to taste with salt and pepper. Pour mixture into a baking dish, and cover with small baking powder biscuits or pastry dough. Bake at 400° for 15 minutes, or until well browned.

1940 BARBECUED STEAKS

In 1940 you could buy a Chrysler Sedan for $995, a 6 cubic foot refrigerator for $112.75, and one of those mix masters with everything but the kitchen sink (as they said in 1940) for $23.75. Barbecuing was a national hobby, and recipes like this one appeared often on the pages of ladies' magazines.

4 tablespoons salt
3 tablespoons pepper
½ clove of garlic
⅔ tablespoon chopped
    rosemary leaves

Beef steaks
Fresh long stemmed parsley
Melted butter
Bay leaves
Water

96

Combine the salt, pepper, and garlic clove (rubbed into the mixture). Add the rosemary and mix well. Rub the entire mixture into the steak you are about to barbecue (on both sides) and let stand for an hour. Brush the seasonings off, and broil. Brush often with the parsley dipped in the melted butter. Soak a couple of bay leaves in water, and when the fire blazes up, sprinkle some of this water over it. This will help flavor the meat.

1938 POT ROAST WITH TOMATO SAUCE

1938 was the same year that Claudette Colbert told the public how emotional acting scenes led her to Luckies; it was the throat strain, she said. You could also sell seeds for your choice of a violin (30 packets), wrist watch (60 packets), or a junior guitar (30 packets), and listen to General Hugh S. Johnson on the NBC Blue Network. It was in 1938 that this recipe was first published. It is the first pot roast I've ever come across that uses mayonnaise.

2 pounds beef shoulder	¼ cup cold water
2 tablespoons hot cooking fat	2 cups canned tomatoes
Salt and pepper to taste	2 tablespoons diced onions
½ cup boiling water	2 tablespoons mayonnaise
2 tablespoons flour	⅛ teaspoon dry mustard

You'll want to use a heavy kettle or Dutch oven for this recipe. Brown the meat in hot fat and season with salt and pepper. Now add the boiling water and cover. Simmer for 2½ hours. Remove the meat and set aside. Combine flour and cold water, shaking well; add it to the broth you cooked your meat in, stirring constantly. Cook, stirring constantly, until thickened and smooth. Now, add the tomatoes, onions, mayonnaise and mustard. Place the meat back in the kettle, and cover. Simmer for another half hour.

1943 BARBECUED BEEF AND POTATO BALLS

In 1943 the average U.S. female was 5'3" tall, weighed 113½, and had a 25½ inch waist, just over her 39 inch hips. So said the bureau of statistics, as we compared ourselves to the movie stars of the day. This barbecue recipe does well in the oven, as well as on an open fire. It comes from a 1943 magazine, which tells us that it is rich in vitamins C and B.

Beef Mixture:

¾ pound ground beef
¼ pound ground pork
1½ cups grated potatoes
½ cup grated onions

¼ cup chopped green pepper
1½ teaspoons salt
¼ teaspoon pepper
¼ cup margarine or butter

Combine the meat, potatoes, onions, green peppers, 1½ teaspoons salt, and pepper; shape mixture into balls. Place in a well-greased pan, and pour the barbecue sauce over the meat.

Barbecue Sauce:

⅔ cup dill pickle juice
⅔ cup chili sauce
4 drops Tabasco
4 teaspoons Worcestershire
    Sauce

1 teaspoon salt
6 tablespoons diced dill pickle

Mix the dill pickle juice, chili sauce, Tabasco, Worcestershire sauce, salt, and dill pickle; pour over meat. Bake at 375° for 30 minutes.

1943 MEAT ROLL-UPS

Although this recipe calls for making your stuffing or dressing from scratch, you can buy commercially prepared products and save yourself some time. It's your choice. To start from the bottom up, you'll need:

1 pound ground beef	1 tablespoon melted butter
1 teaspoon salt	½ teaspoon poultry seasoning
Pepper	½ teaspoon salt
¼ cup water	Pepper
2 cups fine dry bread crumbs	Hot water
2 tablespoons minced onion	

Combine meat, 1 teaspoon salt, pepper, and ¼ cup water; mix thoroughly. Divide the meat mixture into 6 portions and place on waxed paper. Press the portions into 5 x 5-inch squares (you can do this by placing another strip of wax paper over the meat, and rolling it out). Combine the bread crumbs, onion, melted butter, seasonings, and enough hot water to moisten. Put a spoonful of the stuffing in each meat square, and roll up. Put beef roll-ups in a greased baking dish, and bake at 375° for 45 minutes. Serve with Vegetable Sauce.

Vegetable Sauce:

2 cups canned tomatoes	¼ cup chopped onion
½ cup chopped green pepper	Salt and pepper to taste
½ cup chopped celery	

Combine all ingredients in a saucepan; heat to boiling. Simmer for 30 minutes. Serve hot over Meat Roll-Ups.

CECILS

Cecils are meatballs of a sort, named after some long-forgotten someone, I suppose.

1 pint chopped meat	1 tablespoon bread crumbs
1 level teaspoon salt	2 eggs
1 tablespoon minced parsley	Hot fat
⅛ teaspoon pepper	Additional bread crumbs

Mix first 5 ingredients and 1 egg in a bowl; shape mixture into balls. Beat remaining egg; dip the balls into the egg and then into bread crumbs to cover. Fry in hot fat til done. Serve with Tomato Sauce.

Tomato Sauce:

½ pint tomatoes, strained	Flour
1 slice onion	Salt
1 bay leaf	Pepper
Butter	

To make a tomato sauce for your Cecils, heat your tomatoes, onion and bay leaf in a saucepan. Rub the butter and flour together and add them to the tomatoes. Add salt and pepper and continue to heat til blended. Serve with Cecils.

1949 STEAK, COUNTRY STYLE

In 1949 a new washing machine came out that didn't have to be bolted to the floor. Princess Elizabeth was a mere 23, and Milton Berle captivated us all at 8 p.m. on Tuesday nights. That same year this recipe was first published:

2 pounds round steak
Seasoned flour
½ cup butter or margarine, divided
2 medium onions, sliced
½ pound peeled fresh or canned mushrooms, sliced

½ cup water
2 tablespoons grated cheese
1 teaspoon salt
Dash of pepper
¼ teaspoon paprika
¼ cup sour cream

Cut steak into serving pieces and dredge with the seasoned flour. Melt ¼ cup butter in a large frying pan and add the onions and mushrooms. Cook until the onions are tender and the mushrooms are just lightly browned. Remove the onions and mushrooms from the pan and set aside. Add the remaining ¼ cup butter; when melted add the steak and brown on both sides. Stir in the rest of the ingredients along with the mushroom mixture. Cover, and cook until meat is tender enough to cut with a fork. Serves 6.

1933 HAM ROLL

Biscuit dough
2 cups cooked ham (ground or cut into small pieces)

2 cups milk gravy or white sauce

Roll the biscuit dough into an oblong shape, making it about ⅓-inch thick. Spread the ham over it, and moisten with just enough gravy or sauce to do so. Roll up like you would a jellyroll, and put into a greased loaf pan. Bake at 450° for 20 to 25 minutes.

1933 FRANKFRITTERS

Banana Fritters? Sure. Corn Fritters? Of course. But Frank *Fritters? Oh, yes! And they're good too. Back in 1933 they cost just 35¢ a person to prepare. Today they're still an economical dish that the kids will love.*

Hot Dogs:

1 pound hot dogs

2 tablespoons prepared mustard

Prick your hot dogs and cook in boiling water for 10 minutes. Drain. When they are cool, slit them just enough to spread some mustard inside each one. Put them back in their original shape, and set aside.

Batter:

2 eggs
½ cup milk
2 tablespoons vegetable shortening

1 cup flour
1 teaspoon baking powder
½ teaspoon salt
Oil for deep-frying

Beat eggs well; add milk and shortening. Sift your dry ingredients; add them to your egg mixture and beat til well blended. Fill a frying pan (make sure it's nice and deep) ⅔ full with your vegetable oil. When the oil gets hot (about 370°) you're ready. To test the temperature just place a bread cube in the oil and if it browns in 60 seconds, you're ready to continue. Now, dip each hot dog into the batter. Fry your fritters til brown, and drain on paper towels. For an unusual treat, pour hot tomato sauce over them at serving time.

1943 MEAT PUFF

1943 was a time of ration cards, and careful meal planning. This particular dish was sent in by an industrious reader who made the most of what she had.

1½ cups flour	2 teaspoons minced onion
2 teaspoons baking powder	¼ cup grated carrot
½ teaspoon salt	2 tablespoons melted
2 well-beaten egg yolks	shortening
1 cup milk	2 stiffly beaten egg whites
1 to 1½ cups coarsely	
chopped leftover meat	

Pour all of your dry ingredients into a sifter and sift together. Mix your egg yolks and milk together and then add them to the sifted ingredients. Stir well. Add the onion, meat, carrot, and shortening; mix well. Fold in the egg whites. Now pour the entire mixture into a well-greased 1-quart baking dish. Bake at 425° for 45 minutes. You can serve with hot gravy, if you choose. It looks wonderful when served, as it sits on your table with its crusty brown top.

1925 BAKED APPLE WITH SAUSAGE

A man thought this little dish up. It's wonderfully easy—with only two ingredients: apples and sausages.

Core ruddy apples and put a link sausage in each cavity (the little cocktail sausages are perfect!). Bake until the apples are tender and the red skin is cracked. Baste frequently with the fat from the sausage. You might serve this with a baked potato and salad for color.

1948 POLENTA WITH ITALIAN SAUSAGE

This hearty meal incorporates corn meal and Parmesan cheese in its ingredients. The recipe, one of several in the Christmas edition of a magazine, works just as well with bulk sausage meat in place of Italian sausage. (Just shape bulk sausage meat into about 16 patties, and brown slowly. Pour off the fat, and continue as below.)

1 quart water
1 cup yellow corn meal
1 teaspoon salt
1 pound Italian sausage
1 clove garlic, minced
2 tablespoons chopped fresh
  parsley

1 #2 (20-ounce) can
  tomatoes
¼ cup grated Parmesan
  cheese

Combine water, corn meal, and salt in the top of a double boiler, or in a heavy pan; bring to a boil, stirring constantly. Now cover and continue cooking for about an hour and a quarter. Stir once in a while. Now cut the Italian sausage into pieces, and brown slowly in a skillet. Add the garlic to the pan, and continue cooking til the sausage has browned lightly. Add the parsley, and tomatoes, and cover. Simmer for about an hour. Just before serving season with salt and pepper, and spread half of corn meal mush on a hot serving platter. Cover this with half of your sauce, and repeat. Sprinkle with cheese, and use any extra parsley for garnish.

1933 HAMETTES WITH BANANAS

This easy little dish serves six, and makes good use of leftover ham.

3 tablespoons flour
2 tablespoons milk
¼ teaspoon pepper
1 tablespoon onion (minced)
2 cups leftover ground cooked
   ham

2 eggs
6 small bananas
Juice of one lemon
Vegetable shortening

Combine flour, milk, pepper, onion, and ham together. Beat eggs; add to the flour mixture. Fill a frying pan ⅔ full with shortening and heat til a cube of bread will brown in 40 seconds. Drop ham mixture by spoonfuls into the hot shortening and fry until brown. Drain on paper towels. Peel and slice bananas down the center. Dip each banana half in lemon juice and dredge with flour. Fry in another pan of hot shortening til brown. (You can do these two things simultaneously). Drain, and serve with Hamettes.

VEAL CHOPS À LA RICHELIEU

4 veal chops
4 potatoes, cut into little
   rounds
¾ cup beef bouillon

3 or 4 onions, minced
1 clove of garlic
Seasoning

Cover chops in a small Dutch oven with all other ingredients; season with salt and pepper. Heat to the boiling point slowly on stove top. Place in oven and bake at 350° for ¾ of an hour. Serve with the vegetables cooked with veal.

1931 VEAL BIRDS

In 1931 Listerine had people worrying about halitosis, and everyone had their eyes on John and Dolores Barrymore's new baby: Dolores Ethel May. This recipe appeared that same year, and called for a minimum of ingredients, along with a never-fail bread stuffing.

2 cups soft bread crumbs
1 onion, chopped
½ teaspoon salt
⅛ teaspoon sage
⅛ teaspoon pepper
¼ cup melted fat
Water

Thin pieces of veal steaks, cut
    4 x 2-inches long
Toothpicks
Flour
Salt
Pepper
Fat

Make the stuffing first. Mix the first 5 ingredients in a bowl. Add the melted fat and just enough water to moisten slightly; toss together. Spread the stuffing over the veal steaks and roll up; fasten with toothpicks. Dredge the steaks with flour, salt and pepper; place steaks in a frying pan which is filled with hot fat. Sauté the rolls until they are a golden brown. Put into a baking dish (at least 3 inches deep); add water or milk so that half of the steaks (each steak) are covered. Bake at 350° for 30 minutes or til tender. Use the pan drippings liquid for making gravy.

1934 CALIFORNIA PORK AND BEANS

This recipe, first published in 1934, has a surprise ingredient—apple cider. It takes a little planning ahead, as you have to soak the beans overnight, but it's very tasty.

1 cup dried lima beans	Thyme
4 cups cold water	2 large onions, thinly sliced
Salt	6 pork chops
Flour	¾ cup apple cider (or apple
Pepper	juice)

Soak those beans overnight in water that covers them. In the morning, pour off the water and add the four cups of cold water mentioned above, along with the salt (just a pinch will do it). Cover and cook over a low flame for about an hour and a half. Combine flour, salt, pepper, and thyme; rub the pork chops with seasoned flour. Fill a large baking pan with alternate layers of beans and onions. Place the chops on top, and pour cider over the whole thing. Bake at 350° for about an hour. Then turn the chops over, and cook until browned.

Slippery Floors

An old lady who was staying with me was troubled with slipping on my polished floors. We tried fastening a few strips of adhesive plaster to the soles of her shoes and the difficulty was removed.

1927 RICE AND VEAL CUTLETS

1 cup cooked rice
1 cup cold, finely chopped
  veal
¼ cup milk
1 egg, beaten

2 tablespoons butter
½ teaspoon salt
⅛ teaspoon pepper
1 tablespoon chopped parsley
Fine dry bread crumbs

Warm the rice and chopped veal along with the milk in the upper-part of a double-boiler. As mentioned earlier, you can use a heat-dispurser, or heavy metal saucepan when there is no double-boiler in the house. Gradually add the beaten eggs to the veal mixture, stirring constantly. Add butter and seasonings; cook, stirring constantly, until the mixture thickens. Spread this mixture on a shallow plate to cool; when it handles easily, shape it to form cutlets. Roll the cutlets in fine bread crumbs, then egg, and then in crumbs again. Fry each cutlet in hot (375°) deep fat until light and brown. Brush each cutlet with oil, and brown in a hot (400°) oven.

VEAL FIESTAS

Back in 1932, when this dish was first introduced to an economy-minded public, it cost just 62¢ a serving.

1½ pounds veal steak
1 teaspoon salt
⅛ teaspoon pepper
2 tablespoons flour
4 tablespoons shortening

3 large onions, sliced
½ cup chili sauce
1½ cups hot water
½ cup grated cheese
1½ cups cooked macaroni

Try and get the veal from the lower hind shank and have it cut into about 6 very thin slices; or, if you have to, pound them until they are thin. Season with salt and pepper, and then dredge them in flour. Heat your skillet, and add the shortening. Fry the veal quickly in hot shortening until the pieces are brown on both sides. Cover the veal with onions; add chili sauce and hot water. Cover the skillet, cook on a low flame for about 30 minutes, or transfer mixture to a 375° oven and bake for the same amount of time. Remove the cover, and sprinkle with cheese. Put back in oven or on stove just long enough to melt the grated cheese. Remove veal to a platter. Put your cooked macaroni in the same skillet to absorb all the juices, and stir until heated. Serve macaroni and veal together.

1944 SPECIAL DINNER PIE

This recipe from a war-time magazine features a mint crust!

Mint Crust:

1½ cups flour
1½ teaspoons salt

⅔ cup shortening
¾ cup chopped mint leaves

To make the mint pie crust, measure and then sift the flour and salt together. Cut in the shortening until it is evenly blended. Add the chopped mint. If there isn't enough moisture in the mint leaves add a little cold water. Roll out the pastry to fit a 9-inch pie pan. Bake at 425° for 10 minutes. Set pastry aside.

Filling:

2 pounds lamb shoulder cut in
   1-inch cubes
1 teaspoon salt
½ teaspoon pepper
2 tablespoons shortening,
   melted

1 cup water
1 cup sliced mushrooms
2 cups green peas
6 medium carrots, cut in
   strips
8 small white onions, peeled

Season the lamb cubes with salt and pepper and brown them in a frying pan with melted shortening. Add a cup of water, and mushrooms; simmer for 30 minutes. Cook the other vegetables in salted boiling water; when they are done, season them with salt and pepper. Add a little butter for flavoring. Arrange them around your pie shell. Remove the meat and mushrooms from the skillet, and thicken the gravy with a little flour. Pour the gravy over the meat and mushrooms and vegetables, and serve.

SADDLE OF LAMB

I grew up eating all sorts of divine lamb dishes. Lamb chops were my very favorite . . . with enough of them for two people on my plate. I can remember my mother roasting lamb as well, and there is no better smell in the world than that of lamb roasting in the kitchen. Here is a recipe from the early twenties which features a saddle of lamb.

1 teaspoon salt	1 bouillon beef cube
Pepper	3 tablespoons chopped mint
1 saddle of lamb	leaves
4 tablespoons flour	2 tablespoons vinegar
2½ cups boiling water	4 tablespoons butter

Sprinkle salt and pepper all over the meat; dredge meat with flour. Place the lamb in a roasting pan; pour 1½ cups of boiling water around it. Roast at 350° for 1½ hours, basting every 15 minutes or so. While the lamb roasts, dissolve the bouillon cube in the remaining cup of boiling water. Combine bouillon mixture with mint and vinegar; set in a warm place until the lamb is done. Remove the lamb liquid from the pan and add it to the mint and vinegar mixture. Melt the butter in a saucepan, and allow it to brown just slightly, adding the 4 tablespoons flour and browning some more. Pour this over the vinegar-mint-drippings liquid, and stir constantly. Strain, and serve with the lamb.

1944 LAMB PIE (WITHOUT A CRUST)

Ah—remember when lamb was one of the less-expensive meats on your grocery list? Not so any more, and what was once an economical dish, is now a "company" meal. This one's a goodie.

1½ pounds breast or shoulder
   lamb cut into 1½-inch
   pieces
2 tablespoons meat drippings
3 cups water
2½ teaspoons salt

¼ teaspoon pepper
4 carrots, sliced
1 cup lima beans
4 small onions
2 cups cooked mashed
   potatoes

Flour the pieces of lamb by putting the flour in a plastic bag and dropping a few chunks of lamb in at a time til coated lightly. Get out your heaviest frying pan, brown meat lightly on all sides in those meat drippings, for about 15 minutes. Now add three cups of water and your salt and pepper. Cover, and simmer for 1½ hours. Add the vegetables, except mashed potatoes, and cook for about a half hour, or until they are tender. Now, transfer the whole thing to a favorite casserole dish, and top with a circle of mashed potatoes. Place under the broiler for about a minute—just long enough to brown the potatoes. Serves 4.

Beverages

Beverages

PROHIBITION COCKTAIL

During the prohibition years, magazine food editors tried to come up with tempting substitutes for liquor. These recipes are still good, and are creative drinks. On the following pages you'll find all sorts of non-alcoholic thirst-quenchers. For our first recipe from 1931, you'll need:

3 grapefruits

4 oranges

¾ to 1 cup sugar

1 pint grape juice

Gingerale

Red cherries

Peel your grapefruits and oranges and remove all of that white membrane. Break each fruit section into cubes, and place in a bowl; add your sugar, then grape juice and gingerale as desired. Taste for sweetness and make extra sugar additions according to taste. Top with a cherry!

1927 ESKIMO CUP

Back in 1927, people would sit out on their verandas and sip something cool to take away the summer's heat. This is just one of several non-alcoholic drinks offered by a leading magazine to help fight high temperatures!

1 cup grapefruit juice

½ cup lemon juice

½ cup sugar

1 cup water

1 pint gingerale

Cracked ice

Combine the fruit juices, sugar, and water; stir until the sugar is dissolved. Now, add the gingerale and serve over cracked ice. Makes 1¼ quarts.

1937 ORANGE-HONEY SHAKE

M.P.G. was a factor even in 1937. Ford advertised a V-8 that got 22 to 27 miles per gallon. It must have been a "honey" of a car! Sorry about that, but not this . . . it's delicious!

1 cup orange juice
2 teaspoons lemon juice
⅔ cup water
A pinch of salt

⅔ cup evaporated milk
6 tablespoons of honey or ½ cup sugar

Combine all of your juices. Then combine your water, salt and milk. Pour the juices into the milk slowly, stirring constantly. Add the honey or sugar; chill. Tastes even better when poured over cracked ice!

EGG BATTER

6 eggs
1# (3½ cups) sifted
   confectioners sugar

1 tablespoon unflavored gelatin
¼ cup cold water

Separate your eggs and put the yolks aside. Beat the whites until they are almost stiff; add sugar slowly while you continue to beat. Beat egg yolks now until they are thickened and lemon colored. Fold egg yolks into first mixture. Sprinkle your gelatin on top of the cold water and let it soften for 5 minutes. Beat gelatin mixture into the combined egg mixture. Now you are ready to pour it all into a jar, cover, and chill. This egg batter will give body and smoothness to your milk drinks, and it will keep about 2 weeks!

Once again, some pre-tested mixtures for the less adventuresome:

116

1937 "SIRUPS"

Ever hear of "oragene"? Beechnut put it out in 1937. It was a chewing gum with a firmer texture than most—and was supposed to help fight mouth acidity. Their slogan was "Chew with a Purpose." 1937 was a social time for many Americans. Magazines were filled with grooming and entertainment tips.

Ever since I found these wonderful recipes in a favorite 1937 magazine, I've been experimenting with them. They can be mixed and put in jars far ahead of when you'll need them—they keep forever! They're very concentrated, and you won't need much to get the taste you're after. Some are very thick, others have chunky pieces of fruit in them. Mix them with your favorite fruit juices, each other, iced tea, club soda, or gingerale. But try them all! You might want to serve them at a party and let your guests mix and match. They're a great conversation starter!

MINT SIRUP

You'll need:

2 cups of sugar　　　　　　　　**2 tablespoons corn sirup**
20 stalks fresh mint, crushed　**1 cup of water**

Combine all of your ingredients together in a saucepan and stir until your sugar has dissolved. Simmer over low heat for 15 minutes. Strain, pour into a jar, and chill.

LEMON SIRUP

You'll need:

2 cups of sugar
2 tablespoons of corn sirup
1 cup water

3 tablespoons of grated lemon
   rind

Combine all of your ingredients together in a saucepan and stir until your sugar has dissolved. Then simmer over a low flame for 15 minutes. Strain, and pour what's left into a jar. Pop that jar into the refrigerator and it'll keep for months.

MOCHA SIRUP

2½ cups firmly packed dark
   brown sugar

4 cups hot water
2⅔ cups medium-grind coffee

Melt the sugar in a heavy pan over a low flame, and stir constantly until it's a light brown, and rather creamy. Then add your water, and continue stirring until the sugar is dissolved. Add coffee, and cover. *Let it stand for 24 hours.* Then strain it through cheesecloth, and pour into a jar and chill. This makes 4 cups of sirup.

PINEAPPLE SIRUP

This is another one of my favorites!

1 #2 can of crushed
  pineapple (or a medium-
  sized can)
1 tablespoon grated orange
  peel

1 cup water
½ cup sugar
12 whole cloves

Combine all of your ingredients together in a saucepan and stir until your sugar has dissolved. Simmer over a low flame for 15 minutes. *Don't strain!* All of that good crushed fruit is delicious in combinations of sirup and most any fruit drink you can name. Try it with club soda for a real surprise! But do take out the cloves before pouring your sirup into a jar and chilling. (This makes about 3 cups of sirup.) Try a pineapple sirup and brown sugar mixture over fresh fish. Baste often while broiling. It's terrific!

If you're not very adventuresome, here are some pre-tested combinations of the sirups I've just given you. They're good—but after you've tried these—experiment on your own!

SPICE SIRUP

This sirup is wonderful with iced tea, and one of the best "mixers" for other sirups.

2 cups of sugar
2 tablespoons of corn sirup
2 whole cloves
1 cup of water

1 3-inch stick of cinnamon
1 piece whole ginger or 2
  cracked ginger pieces

Combine all of your ingredients together in a saucepan; heat and stir until your sugar has dissolved. Simmer over a low flame for 15 minutes. Strain and pour into a jar, and chill.

LEMONADE

2 or 3 tablespoons of Lemon
Sirup
2 tablespoons lemon juice

⅔ cup ice-water
Ice

This makes one tall glass.

CLOVE LEMONADE

1 pint water
Juice of 6 lemons
1 teaspoon whole cloves

2 cups sugar
Seltzer, water and ice

This is one recipe for lemonade that calls for boiling the water! But before you do, add the lemon juice, cloves and sugar to it. Boil til the sugar dissolves and it makes a syrup. Use 2 tablespoons of the syrup to each glass, filling it up with either seltzer or water and ice.

GRAPEFRUIT PUNCH

2 tablespoons lemon sirup
½ cup grapefruit juice
Ice

1 tablespoon lemon juice
½ cup sparkling water

This makes one tall glass.

Before we leave the wonderful world of "sirups," here are two delicious recipes for guests. The first, a tea punch which will yield 25 half-cup servings. The second, a fruit punch which will yield 12 half-cup servings.

TEA PUNCH

Mix 1¼ cups Lemon Sirup, ¼ cup Spice Sirup, 1 cup Pineapple Sirup, 1¼ cups lemon juice, 6 cups of freshly brewed tea, 1 cup grapefruit juice, 1 cup pineapple juice, and 2 cups of ice water. Add ice.

FRUIT PUNCH

Add ½ cup Mint Sirup, ½ cup Lemon Sirup, ½ cup Pineapple Sirup, ½ cup lemon juice, 1 cup grapefruit juice, and ½ cup grape juice. Add 3 cups of ice water and ice.

1927 CURRANT PUNCH

1 teaspoon ground ginger
1 teaspoon ground cinnamon
Dash of ground nutmeg
3 cups sugar

1 quart fresh currants
Water
Cracked ice

Combine ginger, cinnamon, nutmeg and sugar; add to fresh currants. Cook fifteen minutes; strain and let cool. This is very strong, so serve one part juice and three parts water. Oh—serve over cracked ice if possible!

GRAPEADE

2 tablespoons Spice Sirup
⅔ cup grape juice
1 tablespoon lemon juice

½ cup sparkling water
Crushed ice

This makes one tall glass.

GRAPE GINGER

1 cup sugar
1 quart water
1½ cups grape juice

1 pint gingerale
½ cup lime juice
Cracked ice

Add sugar to water and stir until sugar is dissolved. Then add the next 3 ingredients and serve over ice. Makes 2 quarts.

MINT WALLOP

Some people can't get rid of mint in their back yard—it seems to grow like crazy. If that's the case, this is the drink for you!

6 teaspoons tea
Several sprigs mint
Juice of 4 lemons
Juice of 2 oranges
Grated rind of 4 lemons
Grated rind of 2 oranges

1 quart boiling water
2 cups sugar
1 quart white grape juice
1 quart cold water
Green food coloring

I don't know what they did for white grape juice back in 1927, but now it's available on your supermarket shelf. Everything else should be easy enough to come by. Put the tea, mint, lemon and orange juice from your oranges and lemons, and the grated rind of them into an earthen or enamel pitcher or bowl and pour the boiling water over it. Let cool and then strain through a cheesecloth. Now add your sugar, grape juice, and cold water and stir until the sugar has dissolved. Add just enough coloring (a lot goes a long way) to make the liquid a light green. Pour over ice. Makes 4 quarts.

SPICE TEA

2 tablespoons of Spice Sirup   1 tablespoon lemon sirup
1 tablespoon lemon juice   ¾ cup freshly brewed tea
Ice

This makes one tall glass.

Here are some other sirups from that same 1937 goldmine. In those days there were no premeasured chocolate powders available, or syrups. So, while these don't taste exactly like the chocolate drinks you are accustomed to, they are quite good in their own right. According to ingredients, some last longer than others.

CHOCOLATE BASE

4 squares unsweetened baking   ⅔ cup hot water
   chocolate (4 oz.)   2 egg yolks
1 cup sugar

Melt the squares of chocolate; let them cool until they are lukewarm. Combine sugar and water; cook, stirring constantly, over a low flame until the sugar is dissolved. Cool until it is lukewarm. Beat your egg yolks slightly; add your sirup a little at a time, beating well after each addition. Add chocolate mixture to egg mixture, a little at a time, beating well after each addition. Continue to beat a minute longer until the mixture has thickened. Pour into a jar, and chill!

COCOA BASE

1 cup cocoa
1 cup sugar
¼ teaspoon salt

1 cup cold water
2 teaspoons vanilla extract

Combine your cocoa, sugar, and salt and pour them in a saucepan. Add the water slowly over a low flame. Stir until smooth and then boil for about 2 minutes, while you continue to stir. Add your vanilla, and pour the entire mixture into a jar and chill.

CHOCOLATE NOG MIX

Mix 2 tablespoons of chocolate or cocoa base with 1 tablespoon of your Egg Batter until you get a smooth paste. Then stir in 1 cup of cold milk, and a scoop of vanilla or chocolate ice cream. For a "Mocha Nog" just substitute 2 tablespoons of Mocha Sirup for Chocolate or Cocoa Sirup, and use your choice of vanilla or coffee ice cream.

CHOCOLATE "HIGHBALL"

Start with 2 tablespoons of Chocolate or Cocoa Base in a tall glass. Then pour one half cup of cold milk into your glass very slowly and stir constantly. Add ½ cup of gingerale and stir just enough to mix the two. Then add a scoop of vanilla or chocolate ice cream. To make a "Mocha Highball," just substitute 3 tablespoons of Mocha Sirup for Chocolate Base and use vanilla or coffee ice cream.

Desserts

Desserts

CAKES

1920 THREE EGG ANGEL FOOD CAKE

Angel Food Cakes are one of the forgotten recipes. I remember my grandmother baking them up fresh and cooling them on the back screened porch. I'd come in from playing outside, and she'd have a cool glass of sweet milk waiting, with a wonderfully light piece of angel food cake. Here's a recipe from the early twenties that makes this wonderful cake a little less expensive, since most recipes call for 5 to 8 eggs.

1 cup sugar	⅔ cup scalded milk
1⅓ cups flour	1 teaspoon vanilla or almond
½ teaspoon cream of tartar	extract
3 teaspoons baking powder	Whites of three eggs
½ teaspoon salt	

Mix and sift sugar, flour, cream of tartar, baking powder, and salt four times. Now add your milk slowly, while it's still hot, and beat continuously. Then add vanilla, and mix well. Fold in your egg whites which you have beaten until they were light. When this is well mixed, turn it into an ungreased angel food cake tin. Bake in a very slow oven at 300° for 45 minutes. Remove from the oven, turn upside down, and let it stand until cool. If you wish to ice the cake you'll need:

½ teaspoon butter	1½ cups confectioners sugar
2 tablespoons hot milk	½ teaspoon vanilla extract

This is an easy frosting. Just add your butter to the hot milk, and add your sugar to it slowly until it is spreadable. Then add your vanilla at the last. Spread on the top and sides of the cake. Done!

1935 SURPRISE APPLE CAKE

$18 a week could feed 10 in 1935, capes were the fashion, and since there were no ball points, people wrote with fountain pens. Perhaps they used their $2.50 Waterman to copy this recipe from a favorite magazine. You'll need:

2 cups graham cracker crumbs
2 tablespoons melted butter
½ teaspoon ground cinnamon
3 eggs
1 can (1⅓ cups) sweetened
  condensed milk

2 tablespoons lemon juice
Grated rind of one lemon
2 cups applesauce (which has
  been pushed through a
  sieve)

Mix your graham cracker crumbs, butter and cinnamon; spread about ¼ of crumb mixture in a thick layer on the bottom of a buttered spring mold or deep 10-inch cake pan. Separate your eggs, and beat the yolks well. Add condensed milk, lemon juice, rind, and applesauce to beaten egg yolks. Beat your egg whites til stiff; fold into milk mixture. Pour the whole thing into your cake mold or pan and cover with remaining cracker crumbs. Bake at 350° for 50 minutes.

SUN GOLD COCONUT CAKE
WITH MARSHMALLOW ICING

This cake is a delicious combination of yellow cake, marshmallow icing and shredded coconut. Back in the late twenties, when it was first made, there were no such things as miniature marshmallows, and the original recipe calls for cutting up whole marshmallows into tiny pieces. You can save yourself a lot of time and trouble by just buying the miniatures. To make this delicious cake you'll need:

⅔ cup shortening
2 cups sugar
4 eggs, separated
3 cups pastry flour
3 teaspoons baking powder

1 teaspoon salt
1 cup milk
1 teaspoon vanilla extract
1 cup shredded coconut

Beat the shortening and sugar together until they make a smooth cream. Beat egg yolks until foamy; stir into creamed mixture, then beat until they are very light. In another bowl, sift your dry ingredients together three times; add them alternately with the milk to the creamed mixture. Add vanilla and coconut. Beat egg whites until stiff; carefully fold them into batter. Pour batter into three greased and floured 9-inch cake pans. Bake for 15 to 20 minutes at 350°. Let cool 10 minutes in pan; remove to wire rack and cool completely. When cool, ice with Marshmallow Icing.

Marshmallow Icing:

1¾ cups sugar
½ cup hot water
2 stiffly beaten egg whites
1½ cups miniature
  marshmallows

1 teaspoon vanilla extract
Shredded coconut

Cook sugar and hot water to the soft ball stage, stirring frequently. Pour hot mixture over beaten egg whites, beating constantly, until blended. Add marshmallows, and beat until mixture holds its shape. Add vanilla. Spread icing over cake layers. Sprinkle cake with coconut.

BUTTERLESS CAKE

Oh, the War Years. Articles were being written on how to cook tempting dishes without spending money on things like butter and cream. Here's a butterless cake, devised at that very time to help people all over the country come up with a bit of magic when there didn't seem to be any stardust.

You'll need:

1 egg, separated
⅔ cup sugar
½ cup evaporated milk
1 cup flour

2 level teaspoons baking
   powder
⅛ teaspoon salt
¾ teaspoon lemon extract

Put your egg yolk in a mixing bowl and beat until light; gradually add the sugar and milk while beating continuously. Sift your flour, baking powder, and salt together; set aside. Beat egg white until stiff; fold dry ingredients into egg white. Add egg white mixture and flavoring to sugar-milk mixture, blending well. Pour batter in a prepared 8-inch square pan. Bake in a moderately hot oven (375°) for 30 minutes. Top with Icing.

Icing:

You'll need:

2 tablespoons evaporated milk
1 cup powdered sugar

¾ teaspoon lemon extract

Warm your milk in a small saucepan, and add your flavoring and sugar. If you'd like, you can color the icing with vegetable food coloring.

1920 DEVIL'S FOOD CAKE

Today we have so many different kinds of chocolate cake it's hard to choose between all of the different mixes. But the really good deep devil's food mixes of yesterday seem to show them all up. Here's one from the 1920's.

¼ cup butter
½ cup sugar
6½ tablespoons molasses
¼ cup sour milk
1 egg

2 squares chocolate melted in
   6½ tablespoons boiling
   water
½ teaspoon soda
1½ cups flour
1 teaspoon vanilla extract

Combine all your ingredients, starting with the butter and ending with the vanilla, in the order given above. Mix well. Pour in a loaf pan and bake at 350° for 50 minutes. Frost with whipped cream. Top with sprinkled coconut, if desired.

1918 RAISIN COCOA CAKE

Cocoa . . . there's something not too many of us drink very often. My grandmother would start each day with a hot glass of water. Then she would cook up some steaming cocoa, and serve it with what we called a Kaiser Roll, and sweet butter. It was heavenly. Of course she always had plenty of cocoa on hand, and this was the kind of a cake she could whip up on a moment's notice.

1 egg
1 cup molasses
4 tablespoons cold water
1 teaspoon ground ginger

4 teaspoons cocoa
1½ cups flour
1 teaspoon soda
½ cup raisins

Beat egg until foamy; add molasses, water, ginger, and cocoa; beat until well mixed. Sift together flour and soda; add to the egg mixture, mixing well. Stir in raisins. Grease a 9-inch square pan. Bake at 350° for 60 minutes.

ICE BOX CAKE

Everybody has an absolute favorite cake. This one's mine. First of all, it's quick—and you don't have to use the oven—so it's great in the summertime. Second, it tastes—like heaven—like everything good. Because it's made from everything good. It is a 1927 recipe. I've made some substitutions. I use maraschino cherries for the original candied ones, and I use those pre-packaged strawberry shortcake cups instead of the Lady Fingers. I use a square glass baking pan and put four of the shortcake cups on the first layer, and four on the second. If you make nothing else in this cookbook—make this! It's worth the entire price of the book!!

¾ **pound powdered sugar**
½ **pound butter, softened**
4 eggs
A capful of vanilla extract
8 strawberry shortcake cups
   (or 3 dozen Lady Fingers)

1 small (8¼-ounce) can
   crushed pineapple
Maraschino cherries
A capful of vanilla extract
1 pint whipping cream

Cream the sugar and butter together. Then separate your eggs, and put the whites aside. Add each yolk to the sugar mixture, one at a time, beating well after each addition. Beat egg whites until they are stiff; fold them into your sugar mixture. Now add that capful of vanilla, stirring gently.

This old recipe I found called for lining the bottom of your deep cake pan with paraffin paper. Back in 1927, when the recipe was first published, that was the common word for waxed paper. I use two sheets waxed paper, laid cross-wise, so that there is enough overlap to cover the finished cake. (It makes it so you can lift the finished product out of the pan with no mess at all!) After lining the pan, put in 4 of the shortcake cups. That's layer one. Cover them with half of the filling. That's layer two. Cover layer two with half of the crushed pineapple. That's layer three. You can use whole cherries, or slice them in half—according to your own taste. I use the whole cherry. I drop one in the center of each of the cups

132

and one smack in the middle of the cake. Then one or two extras for good measure here and there. That's layer four. Then I whip up one of the ½ pints of whipping cream, until stiff, using no extra sugar. I spread half of the whipped cream over the cake for layer five. Then I start over and repeat each of the five layers again. I then cover the cake making sure that the waxed paper is hanging over the sides of the pan. Chill overnight! I then open the waxed paper and turn the cake upside down onto a serving plate. Then I whip up the other ½ pint of whipping cream until stiff and spread it over the whole cake. You can garnish the finished product with some maraschino cherries, if you like. It's one of the very best cakes I've ever had—and I haven't found one person who didn't like it!

1933 PLUM CAKE

It was a time of knickered boys, and hoops. A housewife could get by on a food budget of $1 a day and feed a family of three. Imagine how much or how little the ingredients to this cake must have cost back then. This recipe belonged to the author's great-grandmother. Like Plum Pudding, it has no plums. You can substitute raisins for currants if you can't find them.

1½ cups butter, softened
1½ cups sugar
4 eggs
6 cups flour
1 tablespoon baking powder
1⅓ cups currants

1 tablespoon baking powder
¼ cup candied cherries
⅔ cup candied fruit peel
⅔ cup orange juice
   (optional)

Cream your butter and sugar. Then add your eggs one at a time. Beat after each addition until the mixture is thoroughly blended. Measure your flour after you sift it, and then sift half of it again with the baking powder, adding it to the first mixture. Mix well. Now dredge your fruit in the remainder of the flour and mix it with your first mixture. Pour the whole thing into a well-oiled 10-inch tube pan, and bake at 325° for one hour.

Note: This cake tends to be dry. Add orange juice if needed.

1920 FRUIT LAYER CAKE

Here's a basic cake with a wonderful filling made from figs, lemon juice, raisins, almonds, and fruit jelly. To make this beautiful cake you'll need:

⅓ cup shortening	2 cups flour
1 cup sugar	4 teaspoons baking powder
1 egg, separated	⅛ teaspoon salt
1 teaspoon vanilla extract	1 cup milk

Cream your shortening well. Add the sugar, yolk of one egg, and vanilla; mix well. Sift together flour and baking powder and salt; add to creamed mixture with milk, mixing well. Beat egg white until stiff; fold beaten egg white into batter. Pour batter into 3 greased cake tins. Bake in a quick oven (400°) about 15 minutes or until cake tests done. When cool, put layers together with the following fruit filling:

Filling:

½ cup fruit jelly	2 tablespoons cornstarch
1½ cups water	Juice of half a lemon
½ cup raisins	½ cup blanched almonds (or
½ pound chopped figs	other nuts)
2 tablespoons sugar	

Cook jelly, water, fruit, and sugar several minutes. Add 2 tablespoons of cornstarch, which you have dissolved in a little water. Cook slowly until it's nice and thick, then remove from the fire. Add lemon juice and nuts and cool. Spread filling between layers of cake. Cover top and sides of cake with frosting.

Frosting:

2 tablespoons hot milk	1½ cups confectioners sugar
½ teaspoon butter	½ teaspoon vanilla extract

Combine hot milk and butter, stirring until butter is melted. Add the sugar very slowly, beating constantly, until you have made a paste that is the right spreading consistency. Add vanilla; mix well. (Double frosting, if necessary, to cover cake.) Spread frosting on top and sides of your cake. If you wish, you can place English walnut halves on top of the cake while the icing is still soft.

THANKSGIVING FRUITCAKE

Here's an unusual fruitcake calling for figs and fruit juice! There are lots of other good things packed into this delicious cake. If you're an experimenter, you might like to try this off-the-beat recipe that came out just in time for Thanksgiving back in 1928. To make it you'll need the following:

1 cup oil
1 cup firmly packed brown
  sugar
4 egg yolks
2 teaspoons ground allspice
2 teaspoons ground cinnamon
1 teaspoon ground cloves
2 teaspoons salt
1 teaspoon baking powder
3 cups flour

1 cup fruit juice
1½ cups chopped candied
  cherries
1 cup shaved citron
1 cup chopped figs
1 cup chopped candied
  pineapple
1 cup raisins
3 cups chopped nuts
4 egg whites, stiffly beaten

Mix the oil, sugar, egg yolks in a large mixing bowl; beat well for about 2 minutes. Sift all of the spices together; add salt, baking powder, and 2 cups flour. Add flour mixture alternately with the fruit juice to the first mixture. Now mix the fruit and nuts with the remaining cup of flour; add to batter. Fold beaten egg whites into the batter mixture. Pour batter into a 10-inch tube pan. Bake at 275° for four hours.

HONEY NUT CAKE

This recipe was created during the war years, when sugar was scarce and people didn't have a lot of money to spend on sweets. It was originally a Christmas cake—but it's good all year long.

2 cups cake flour
2 teaspoons baking powder
½ teaspoon salt
⅔ cup butter
½ cup sugar

½ cup honey
3 eggs
1 cup chopped nuts
¼ cup milk
1 teaspoon vanilla extract

Sift flour and then measure. Add your baking powder and salt to flour and sift together 3 times. Cream your butter until light; gradually add sugar, and cream well. Next comes your honey—add it a third at a time, beating well after each addition. Add about ¼ of your flour mixture and beat until well blended and smooth. Next you'll want to beat your eggs until they are thick enough to pile up in a bowl. Add eggs to your cake mixture. Stir in nuts. Finally, you'll want to add your remaining flour mixture, again in thirds, alternately with your milk, (by adding milk in halves), beating very well after each addition. Stir in vanilla. Pour batter into a 9-inch buttered tube pan. Bake at 325° for an hour and 5 minutes. Frost with this delicious Honey Butter Frosting.

Honey Butter Frosting:

2 tablespoons butter, softened
2 tablespoons honey
⅓ cup sifted confectioners
   sugar
Dash of salt

1 egg white
½ teaspoon vanilla extract
2 cups sifted confectioners
   sugar

Cream butter until light; add honey and blend well. Add ⅓ cup of confectioners sugar and cream very well; add salt. Add egg white alternately with the two cups of sifted confectioners sugar, beating well after each addition. Add vanilla, mixing well, and you've got a cup of frosting. You may want to taste the finished product and see if it's sweet enough for you. If not, add a little more sugar.

Remember, this was a war-time recipe, and they had to be stingy with their sugar. Today our tastes are a little richer. Spread frosting on top and sides of cake.

1921 BUTTERSCOTCH LAYER CAKE

Here's a delicious cake that is beautiful to look at as well as to eat! It's from a 1920 magazine, and is made from the basic ingredients any good cook has on hand.

½ cup butter, softened
1 cup sugar
2 eggs, separated
⅔ cup milk

2 cups flour
3 teaspoons baking powder
¼ teaspoon salt
1 teaspoon vanilla extract

Cream butter until light; gradually add the sugar and beaten egg yolks, mixing well. Add milk, a little at a time, until it has all been added and well mixed. Sift the flour, baking powder, and salt together; add to creamed mixture, mixing well. Add vanilla (or your favorite flavoring). Beat egg whites until stiff; fold into batter. Pour batter in 2 greased layer tins. Bake in a moderate oven (350°) for 25 minutes. When cooled, fill and frost cake with Butterscotch Filling and Icing.

Butterscotch Filling and Icing:

2 cups light corn syrup
½ cup butter

½ cup milk
Chopped nuts

Boil your syrup, butter, and milk together until it forms a soft ball when you drop a bit into cold water. Cool for a few moments WITHOUT STIRRING, and then pour it, while still warm, on the cake. Chopped nuts complete the picture, as you add them while the icing is still soft.

1931 PLANTATION MARBLE CAKE

Radio was in its hayday, with the Camel Quarterhour being a favorite show. You could hear Morton Downey and Tony Wons play your favorite songs. Dorothy Dix gave advice in newspapers across the country and marble cake was very much the thing to bake. This 1931 recipe calls for cake flour.

2 cups sifted cake flour
2 teaspoons baking powder
¼ teaspoon salt
½ cup butter, softened
1 cup sugar
2 eggs, slightly beaten

½ cup milk
½ teaspoon ground nutmeg
1 teaspoon ground cinnamon
½ teaspoon ground cloves
2 tablespoons molasses

Combine sifted flour, baking powder and salt; sift together 3 times and set aside. Cream butter well; add the sugar gradually, beating until light and fluffy. Add eggs to creamed mixture, a little at a time, alternately with your milk. You'll want to beat well after each addition. When the batter is smooth, divide it into 2 parts. Add your spices and molasses to 1 part. Pour or spoon both batters (light and dark) alternately, 1 at a time, into a greased 8-inch square pan. Bake at 350° for 50 minutes. Frost as desired.

1928 AWARD WINNING GOLD CAKE

I guess Bake-Offs have been going on forever. Here's a cake that won over hundreds of entrys, using ingredients you're bound to have on hand most any time. The orange extract is optional, but it makes a nice complement to the flavor of the cake. To make this award-winner you'll need:

2 cups sifted cake flour
3 teaspoons baking powder
½ cup butter, softened
1 cup sugar
3 egg yolks beaten til thick
   and lemon-colored

¾ cup milk
1 teaspoon vanilla or ½
   teaspoon orange extract

This recipe calls for all measurements to be level. So sift your flour, then measure, and then add your baking powder, and sift the flour and powder together three times. Cream your butter well; slowly add your sugar, and cream til the mixture is light and fluffy. Now, add your beaten egg yolks, mixing well. Alternate adding your flour mixture with your milk, a little at a time, beating well after each addition. When the batter is smooth, add the flavoring and beat well. Pour the finished batter into a well greased 8-inch square baking pan. Bake at 350° for 50 to 60 minutes.

1933 LADY GREGORY'S BARM BRACK

I've always loved the name of this Christmas-sy cake. It's perfect for someone who loves everything about fruitcake but the spices. You'll need:

1 cake yeast	5 cups flour
1 cup lukewarm milk (105 to	1½ cups currants
110°)	⅓ cup candied fruit peel,
3 eggs, well beaten	chopped
½ cup softened butter	Grated rind of 1 lemon
1 teaspoon salt	⅔ cup sugar

Combine yeast, milk, eggs, butter, and salt; mix well. Sift your flour (measure flour after sifting) and add it to the first mixture. Beat and knead until smooth. Place dough in a well-greased bowl, then cover with a damp cloth. Let rise in a warm place for 1 hour. Add currants, candied peel, rind, and sugar. Mix thoroughly. Pour into a well-oiled pan, and let rise another half hour. Bake at 375° for 1 hour.

SUNSHINE CAKE

This is one of those cakes I love because I usually have everything I need to make it without rushing to the market. It calls for:

3 tablespoons shortening	1½ cups flour
¾ cup sugar	3 teaspoons baking powder
3 egg yolks, beaten until	½ cup milk
thickened	White Icing
1 teaspoon vanilla, lemon, or	
almond extract	

Cream your shortening; add sugar gradually, beating until fluffy. Add egg yolks; mix well. Now add the flavoring (take your choice . . . I am a vanilla purest myself). Sift flour and baking powder together; add flour mixture alternately with milk to the first mixture, adding each a little at a time. Pour batter into a greased loaf pan. Bake in a moderate oven, (350°), for 35 to 45 minutes. When cooled, cover with White Icing (See recipe for Angel Food Cake).

SPONGE CAKES

Sponge cake is one of those forgotten cakes that was a staple for many years. This particular recipe is for LITTLE SPONGE CAKES and goes back to 1927. It was a time for Hoosier cabinets and Madonna hairdos (hair parted in the middle, straight or loosely waved and caught in a neat chignon—remember that word—at the back of the neck.) "The Bob" was still worn as well. The cook of 1927 had her choice of several kinds of stoves. There were oil cook stoves where you had to turn the wick until yellow tips showed 1½" high above the blue area. Oil-air stoves, which focused on intense blue flame directly against your pot or pan, along with coal stoves and so on. A good many of these stoves were still without oven controls, and so the baking instructions are rather vague. Since a slow oven is called for, I suggest 325°.

2 tablespoons lemon juice	1 tablespoon baking powder
3 eggs, separated	⅛ teaspoon salt
½ cup sugar	A capful of vanilla or lemon
½ cup flour	flavoring

Beat your lemon juice and egg yolks together until they are very thick and light in color. Whip your egg whites until they are nice and stiff and then whip your sugar into them. Fold egg yolks into this mixture. Sift the flour with the baking powder and salt and then add them to your egg mixture. Flavor with whatever extract or flavoring you've chosen. Pour batter into a 10-inch tube pan. Bake in a slow oven at 325°, for one hour. Check at 45 minutes, and then at one hour for doneness.

Note: You can sprinkle confectioners sugar on the finished cake for an extra special treat!

PIES AND TARTS

FRUIT AND CUSTARD TARTS
WITH MERINGUE

This 1925 recipe can be made by the scratch method or convenience method. How convenient it can be is up to you. You can make your own tart shells, or buy them at the store. You can use this recipe for custard, or buy the boxed custard mixes (bake or non-bake). It's all up to you. At any rate, after you have gotten past the shells themselves, here's what you'll need to make the filling—from scratch:

1 cup unsweetened evaporated milk	½ cup sugar
½ cup water	1 teaspoon vanilla extract
3 eggs, separated	About 18 baked tart shells
½ teaspoon salt	Favorite fresh fruit
⅓ cup flour	4 tablespoons sugar

Scald your milk and water in a double-boiler or heavy enameled pan. Beat the egg yolks until thickened; beat in salt, flour and sugar. Stir a small amount of hot milk into yolk mixture until warmed; add yolk mixture to remaining milk, stirring constantly. Cook, stirring constantly, for 15 minutes or until it becomes thick and smooth. When the 15 are up remove from the fire, and let cool. Add the vanilla and stir. Pour filling into the tartlett shells. When the custard sets, top each tart with fresh strawberries, raspberries, banana slices, peach slices or whatever; cover with a meringue made by beating egg whites with 4 tablespoons of sugar.

1920 STRAWBERRY CREAM PIE

Here's a 1920 recipe that calls for a quart of fresh strawberries. In the South, you can pick these strawberries for fun and profit—that is, you can pick them yourselves and save a lot of money, having a good time while doing it. For this recipe you'll need:

¾ cup flour
⅛ teaspoon salt
¼ cup butter
Cold water
1 quart fresh strawberries

¼ cup sugar
½ cup evaporated milk,
   chilled and stiffly whipped
or 1 cup whipping cream

Combine flour and salt in a medium bowl; cut in butter until mixture resembles crumbs. Add enough cold water to form a stiff dough. Shape dough into a ball. Roll out dough until it is ¼-inch thick to fit a 9-inch pie pan. Prick the crust with a fork. Place pastry on an inverted pie pan. Bake at 475° until browned; let cool. Fill the shell with your fresh strawberries, and sprinkle with sugar. Cover with whipped milk or, if you want to add a few more calories and get a little more modern, and whip up a half pint of whipped cream with sugar to your taste, and put on the pie.

1932 RAISIN NUT PIE

In 1932, Harlow was tied up with a chewing gum company (showing us the benefits of exercising our jaws) and ladies were thrilled with this recipe, which calls for just a few ingredients.

1 cup chopped English
   walnuts
½ cup cream
¼ cup firmly packed brown
   sugar

1 cup chopped raisins
1 pinch of salt
2 tablespoons lemon juice
Unbaked 9-inch pastry shell

Combine first 6 ingredients; and pour into a pastry-lined pie pan (or pastry shell). Bake at 425° until crust is crisp and evenly browned.

CORN FLAKE PASTRY

Usually, a cereal company will put out a bunch of recipes to entice consumers to try their cereal. Not so in this case. This recipe comes from a corn-flakes fan, who recommends that you cover the pastry with a "No-Bake" Lemon Chiffon Filling.

Pastry:

4 cups corn flakes cereal	**½ teaspoon ground cinnamon**
¼ cup sugar	**¼ melted butter or margarine**

Roll the corn flakes to make 1 cup of fine crumbs. Add sugar, cinnamon, and melted butter to crumbs; stir well. Press mixture firmly into an 8-inch pie tin. Fill with Lemon Chiffon Filling.

Lemon Chiffon Filling:

1½ teaspoons unflavored gelatin	**½ teaspoon salt**
¼ cup water	**½ cup lemon juice**
1 cup sugar, divided	**1 teaspoon grated lemon rind**
	4 eggs, separated

Put gelatin in a bowl; pour ¼ cup water over it. Set aside. Combine ½ cup sugar, salt, lemon juice and rind; set aside for 5 minutes. Beat the egg yolks until thickened; add to the sugar mixture. Cook over low heat in a heavy pan or over a double-boiler and stir until thick. Remove from heat. Add the gelatin mixture and stir until it dissolves. Cool. Now beat the whites of those eggs until they are stiff, adding a little sugar at a time until you have added ½ cup sugar. Add to mixture. Pour the mixture into the corn flake crust and refrigerate for three hours.

1944 MAPLE CUSTARD PIE

You'll need:

Pie Crust:

1⅓ cups flour
½ teaspoon salt
¼ teaspoon baking powder
½ cup shortening

⅓ cup walnuts, chopped
2 tablespoons water
1 tablespoon vinegar

To make the pie crust in this 1944 recipe, sift the flour, salt, and baking powder together. Cut in shortening until it has been evenly mixed. Stir in chopped walnuts. Combine water and vinegar; add just enough to flour mixture to make a stiff dough. Place dough in a 9-inch pie tin and flute edges.

Filling:

4 slightly beaten eggs
¾ cup maple syrup
¼ teaspoon salt

3 cups milk, scalded
½ teaspoon maple flavoring

Beat the eggs slightly, then add your maple syrup and salt. Gradually stir in the scalded milk. Add flavoring. Pour the mixture into your unbaked pie shell. Bake at 450° for 10 minutes; reduce heat to 350° and bake 25 to 30 minutes longer or until the custard is set. Make sure the pie is cool before serving.

1933 PEACH BUTTERSCOTCH PIE

Everybody has an "I remember when _____cost" they like to relate to others about rising prices. For some it's gasoline or candy bars. For others it's cigarettes. In 1933 cork-tipped Raleighs sold for 15¢ a pack. Even then it was healthier to eat this pie, than smoke those cigarettes. For one large, or two small pies, you'll need:

Your favorite pastry for a double-crusted pie
6 large or 8 small fresh peaches
¾ cup firmly packed brown sugar

3 tablespoons flour
⅓ cup light corn syrup
⅓ cup soft butter
1 tablespoon lemon juice
⅛ teaspoon almond flavoring

Prepare your favorite pastry for a lattice-topped pie. Scald and peel your peaches. Cut them into halves and arrange them, cut side up, in your unbaked pastry lined pie tin. Place pie shell in the refrigerator. Combine next 5 ingredients in a saucepan, stirring well. Cook over low heat, stirring constantly, for just a minute; remove from heat. Add almond flavoring. Let cool just slightly, then pour this over the peach halves. Top with lattice-top crust. Bake at 450° for 15 minutes. Reduce the temperature to 350° and bake 30 minutes more.

Honey In the Comb

To separate honey from the comb, cut off the wooden frame, place in a pan in a slow oven to melt. The wax will rise to the top and when cold may be lifted off in a cake like paraffin. The honey will be perfectly clear.

1930 BUTTER PIE

In 1930, Woolworth's was still a five and ten cents store, women were trying to break the "tub habit" in favor of washing machines, and gas ranges were getting a whole new look. This prize-winning recipe from a now defunct magazine smacks of nostalgia.

½ cup sugar
1 egg
1 heaping tablespoon butter
1 heaping tablespoon flour

1 cup milk
Unbaked pastry for a 9-inch pie

Cream the first four ingredients together until light; add milk and mix well. Pour filling into a deep pie tin lined with unbaked pastry. Bake at 350° for about 30 minutes, or until done.

1932 GRAPE PIE AND GRAPE-SKIN PIE

*Here are two recipes from New York State, which were a part of a wonderful recipe grouping in a 1932 magazine. The grape skin pie, we are told, is considered by real grape connoisseurs as the better of the two. Peeling grapes isn't anyone's idea of fun, but the results are worth the effort. For **GRAPE PIE** you will need:*

2½ cups grape pulp and skins
¾ cup sugar
2 tablespoons flour

3 tablespoons melted butter
Pastry for a 10-inch pie

Wash the ripe grapes. Separate the skins and the pulp. Cook the pulp very slowly until it is soft; rub pulp through a sieve. Combine the sieved pulp and skins; set aside. Combine sugar and flour; add to the grape mixture. Stir in butter. Pour filling into an unbaked pastry-lined 10-inch pie pan. Bake at 425° for 25 minutes.

GRAPE SKIN PIE

2 to 2½ cups grape skins and
juice drained from pulp
1 cup sugar

1½ tablespoons flour
Pastry for a double-crust
10-inch pie

Wash the grapes and press out the pulp. Now drain the juice from this pulp onto the skins and discard the pulp. Combine sugar and flour; add to the skins and juice. Place grape mixture into a 10-inch pie pan lined with pastry and cover with a top crust. Bake at 350° for 45 minutes.

CARROT PIE

Here's another carrot recipe you'll like. It calls for:

2 medium carrots, peeled and
sliced
½ cup sugar
2 eggs, well beaten
1½ cups milk

½ teaspoon ground ginger
½ teaspoon ground cinnamon
Pinch of salt
Pie crust or pastry to make 1
9-inch pie

Cook your carrots until they are almost transparent and tender; drain and mash them. Add sugar, eggs, milk, spices, and salt. Blend well. Pour filling into an unbaked pastry shell. Bake at 350° for 40 minutes. This makes one 9-inch pie.

1921 PRUNE PIE

When this recipe was first introduced, you could not buy "pitted" prunes. You had to do the pitting yourself, after the prunes had been boiled. Today we are lucky, in that the prunes are all pitted and ready to cook. To make this pie you will need the following:

148

2 cups pitted prunes
Cold water
Pastry for a double crust
   9-inch pie
1 tablespoon flour

⅓ cup sugar
½ teaspoon grated lemon rind
   and juice
1 tablespoon butter

Cut the prunes in half, and cover with cold water; allow them to soak for 2 hours. Cook prunes in the same water until they are tender; drain and cool them. Line a 9-inch pie plate with pastry; fill with prunes. Mix the flour and sugar together and sprinkle the mixture over the prunes. Top with lemon juice and grated rind. Dot with butter. Top with upper crust. Bake in a hot (425°) oven for 25 minutes.

1943 SOUR CREAM PLUM PIE

This is a seasonal recipe and it comes from a wartime magazine filled with shortening savers, sugar savers and time savers. The year was 1943, and the pie was—excellent! To recreate this pie you'll need:

½ cup cooking plums
1 egg
½ cup sugar
½ cup sour cream
2 tablespoons lemon juice

⅛ teaspoon salt
⅛ teaspoon ground nutmeg
Pastry for a double-crusted
   9-inch pie

Pit and peel your plums; cut them into tiny pieces and set aside. Beat the eggs until foamy; add sugar and keep beating this mixture until it's nice and light. Next, whip the sour cream into the egg mixture, folding it in first. Add plums, lemon juice, salt and nutmeg; mix well. Now you can either use a ready-made pastry crust or make your own, and pour the filling into it. Cover with a top crust. Be sure and crimp the edges to seal the fruit inside. Bake in a preheated 450° oven for just 5 minutes; reduce the heat to 375° and bake for 40 minutes more. This pie tastes best cold. Try a dip of your favorite ice cream on top for an extra treat!

COOKIES

SOUR CREAM MOLASSES COOKIES

3½ or 4 cups flour
1 teaspoon salt
1 teaspoon baking soda
1 teaspoon ground ginger
2 teaspoons ground cinnamon
½ teaspoon ground cloves
½ teaspoon ground nutmeg

¾ cup shortening
¾ cup firmly packed brown
   sugar
1 egg
¾ cup molasses
¾ cup sour cream
1 cup raisins

Sift together first 7 ingredients; set aside. Cream shortening and sugar together until light; add egg, and beat it (you know the old joke). Anyway, add the molasses and sour cream, mixing well. Add the dry ingredients; mix well. Add raisins (I hope you didn't try and sift them with the dry ingredients). Drop the mixture, by spoonfuls, onto a greased cookie sheet. Bake at 375° for 15 minutes. Makes 3 dozen rather large cookies.

1940 VANILLA KIPFERLN
(CRESCENTS)

Here's a recipe from 1940, the year "Gone With the Wind" became a motion picture. Our recipe calls for vanilla sugar used to roll baked cookies in. You can easily make this by breaking a vanilla bean into pieces and scraping out the inside into a cup of powdered sugar. Let it stand at least 24 hours. The sugar will have black specks in it, so don't worry. That's the way it should look! Now, here's that recipe for Kipferln. You'll need:

3½ ounces (⅔ cup) blanched
   almonds
2¾ cups sifted cake flour
1 cup (½ pound) butter,
   softened

1 teaspoon vanilla extract
¼ cup granulated sugar

150

Use blanched almonds if you can find them, otherwise blanch them yourself; grind almonds in your blender. Combine all ingredients and mix them like you would mix a pie crust pastry, with your fingers or pastry blender. This should make a light pastry dough. Put dough in the refrigerator for about ¾ of an hour. Cut off pieces of dough about the size of a walnut, and shape them into little crescents about 2″ long. Place on an ungreased cookie sheet. Bake at 350° for 10 to 15 minutes or until browned. Roll cookies in your vanilla sugar. You'll get 50 to 60 crescents per recipe.

1948 POPCORN COOKIES

When this recipe was first published in 1948, a dozen popcorn cookies cost just 26¢ to make. This recipe bakes up about 2 dozen cookies, but I'd carry a little more than a fifty-cent piece to the grocery store if I were you.

2 egg whites (beaten til stiff while adding the sugar below gradually)
⅔ cup sugar
4 teaspoons margarine or butter, melted

1½ cups minced popped corn
½ teaspoon salt
1 teaspoon vanilla extract
1 small package blanched almonds, toasted

Beat egg whites until soft peaks form; gradually add sugar, beating constantly until stiff peaks form. Set aside. Combine margarine and popped corn together; fold in beaten egg whites. Add salt and vanilla. Drop batter by teaspoonfuls on to a well-greased cookie sheet. Decorate with nuts. Bake at 325° for 7 minutes.

1942 TOFFEE COOKIES

If you listened to the radio in 1942, you'd hear Bing Crosby—if you went to the movies, you'd see Monty Wooley, Bette Davis, Jimmy Durante, and Reginald Gardiner,—and if you read any magazines, you just might have seen and tried these wonderful cookies.

2 cups cake flour
½ teaspoon cream of tartar
½ teaspoon salt
½ teaspoon baking soda
1 cup firmly packed brown
  sugar

½ cup bacon fat
1 egg, beaten
1 teaspoon vanilla extract
1 cup chopped nuts

Sift your flour first, and then measure it. Add cream of tartar, salt, and soda; sift mixture once more. Blend your sugar and bacon fat by creaming them together. Then add your beaten egg and vanilla; mix thoroughly. Now add dry ingredients, mixing well. Add the nuts last. When everything is well mixed, shape your mixture into a roll, and wrap it in waxed paper; chill for several hours or overnight. Cut chilled roll into thin slices, and place on a cookie sheet. Bake at 275° for 8 to 10 minutes. Cool on wire rack. Makes 2 dozen.

PUDDINGS

1920 RICE PUDDING

This was just one of several magazine recipes which used "sirups" instead of sugar.

5 tablespoons raw long grain
  rice
4 cups milk
½ cup cane sirup

½ teaspoon salt
½ teaspoon ground cinnamon
½ cup raisins

Wash the rice. Mix rice with milk, sirup, salt, cinnamon and raisins. Grease a pudding dish (actually vegetable oil would do just as well); pour pudding into dish. Bake slowly, at 250°, for three hours, stirring often to prevent sticking during the first hour. Serve hot or cold.

INDIAN PUDDING

There is a famous restaurant in Boston that has been around for what seems like forever. They make the most delicious Indian Pudding! Actually, it isn't the kind of a dessert you find on every menu. Here is a recipe for an old fashioned Indian Pudding which is very similar to the one this restaurant is known for, and if you have never tasted it, make sure it is on your "things to be done" list.

1 pint water	¼ teaspoon ground ginger
1 pint evaporated milk	1 cup finely chopped suet
½ cup corn meal	⅔ cup corn syrup
¼ teaspoon salt	⅓ cup molasses

Combine water and milk; scald half of it. Combine corn meal, salt, and ginger in a separate bowl; stir in the suet. Wet the meal and the suet with remaining cup of cold milk; stir well. Add meal mixture to the hot milk, stirring constantly, and cook until thickened. When it is thick, remove from fire to cool a minute; stir in corn syrup, molasses, and the remaining 1 cup of cold milk. Bake 4 hours in a very slow oven (275°) until done. It can be served hot or cold, and with or without whipped cream. Serves 6.

INDIAN PUDDING RECIPE #2

Indian Pudding was very popular in the twenties, and here's a similar recipe which gives you a choice of sorghum or molasses and uses whole milk instead of evaporated milk. The ingredients vary just slightly, and I thought you might like a choice.

2 cups boiling water
1 cup corn meal
4 cups hot milk

½ cup molasses or sorghum
1 teaspoon salt
1 teaspoon ground ginger

Pour the boiling water over the corn meal, then add this to the hot milk and cook in a double-boiler for 20 minutes. Remove from heat. Add the molasses or sorghum, salt, and ginger, stirring well. Pour mixture into a greased pudding dish. Bake at 250° for two hours. Serve with milk, cream, or ice cream.

BUTTERMILK CRUMB PUDDING

Here's a steamed pudding that takes us back to the early 1920's. In those days steamed puddings were very popular, and this one calls for delicious things like raisins and buttermilk.

3 tablespoons shortening
1 cup sugar
2 cups toasted bread crumbs
1½ teaspoons grated nutmeg

1 cup raisins
1 cup buttermilk
1 teaspoon baking soda

Cream shortening until light, gradually add sugar, beating until fluffy. Add bread crumbs, nutmeg and raisins, stirring well. Combine buttermilk and soda; add to raisin mixture, mixing well. Pour batter into a well-oiled pudding mold that is equipped with a lid for steaming. Fill mold two-thirds of the way full. Cover with lid, and steam for 45 minutes. Remove from mold and serve with whipped cream or hard sauce.

1923 CARROT PUDDING

My mother always told me carrots were good for the eyes. I never really knew much more than that about them until I read an article in a 1923 woman's magazine. There I learned that carrots are in the starchy vegetable category along with potatoes, onions, and rice. The next time you boil your carrots save the water, and use it in a cream sauce or soup stock! Here's a pudding that will make your eyes light up. You'll need:

1 cup flour
½ cup firmly packed brown
  sugar
1 cup raisins
½ cup suet, very finely
  chopped
½ cup very finely chopped
  carrot

½ cup potato, very finely
  chopped
1 teaspoon baking soda
⅓ cup chopped nuts
½ teaspoon ground nutmeg
1 teaspoon ground cinnamon
½ teaspoon ground cloves

(In the old days you had to put the carrots and potato (raw) through a food chopper. Now you can use your cuinsart or whatever.) Combine all ingredients, mixing well. Pour into an oiled pudding mold; cover. Steam for about 2 hours. Remove from mold and serve with Hard Sauce.

1923 DATE WALNUT PUDDING

With all the instant desserts available these days, it isn't often you get to taste homemade pudding.

2 eggs

¾ cup sugar

2 tablespoons flour

1 teaspoon baking powder

1 cup chopped walnuts

1 cup chopped dates

Ground cinnamon

First you're going to have to get out a good-sized mixing bowl and beat the eggs well. Gradually add sugar, beating constantly until thickened. Sift flour, and baking powder together; stir in walnuts and dates. Combine dry ingredients with the first mixture. Pour the batter into a well-greased pan, and sprinkle with cinnamon as desired. Bake in a slow oven, 300°, for about 35 minutes. This pudding tastes even better with a generous topping of whipped cream or vanilla ice cream!

1928 FRUITED INDIAN PUDDING

With Christmas just behind them, the editors from this particular woman's magazine wanted something to top their regular Christmas recipes. Everyone was tired of cookies and cakes, and so a pudding seemed to be in order. And here are the ingredients, in order—of appearance.

1 quart milk

½ cup corn meal

1 cup molasses

1 teaspoon salt

½ cup dried figs

½ cup puffed raisins

You'll want to scald the milk and add the corn meal. Cook in a heavy enameled pan, or double-boiler for 15 minutes, stirring constantly. Remove from heat. Add the remaining ingredients, stirring well. Pour mixture into a well-greased pan or baking dish. Bake at 300° about 3½ hours. Serves 8.

1920 COLD CHOCOLATE-CRUMB PUDDING

If you are a baking family, and have cakes on hand often, you'll want to take advantage of the leftover crumbs for this delicious bit of nostalgia.

1 cup mixed cake and bread
  crumbs
2 cups milk
1½ squares unsweetened
  chocolate, melted and
  cooled
¾ cup sugar

3 egg yolks, well beaten
2 tablespoons melted butter
¼ teaspoon salt
½ teaspoon vanilla extract
3 egg whites
½ cup powdered sugar

Soak cake and bread crumbs in 1½ cups milk in the top portion of a double-boiler. Stir melted chocolate and ¾ cup sugar into crumb-milk mixture. Cook, over boiling water until mixture makes a smooth paste. Beat egg yolks, ½ cup milk, butter and salt together until thickened. Gradually stir the egg mixture into the hot mixture, stirring constantly, and cook until mixture is thickened. Remove from heat; add vanilla. Pour mixture into a greased pudding dish. Bake at 325° for 25 minutes. Meanwhile, make meringue by beating egg whites until soft peaks form; gradually add powdered sugar to whites, and beat until stiff. When the baked pudding has cooled slightly, spread meringue over top. Bake at 425° for 5 minutes or until meringue is light brown. Chill before serving.

1928 APPLE RICE PUDDING

This recipe was in a cluster of recipes designed to please children. The idea of rice and apples, plus a hint of orange marmalade makes it a treat for their parents as well.

1½ cups milk
½ cup water
½ cup uncooked rice
2 tablespoons sugar
¼ teaspoon salt
1 tablespoon butter

4 or 5 medium-sized apples, pared and quartered or canned stewed applies
2 to 3 tablespoons orange marmalade

Combine milk and water in a double-boiler or enameled pan. Stir in rice. Steam all until rice is tender. Remove from heat. Stir in sugar, salt, and butter with, of all things, a fork! Stew your apples (or use already stewed apples in a can or jar) by putting them in a little water and cooking over a low flame til soft. Now line a buttered dish with half of the rice; place cooked apples in the center. Spread the marmalade over the apples and rice. Top with remaining rice. Bake at 350° for 30 minutes. Serve with milk or cream.

JAM COTTAGE PUDDING

All measures should be level.

1 cup jam or marmalade
   (any kind)
1 egg, well beaten
1 cup milk

2 tablespoons melted butter
2 cups flour
3 teaspoons baking powder
1 teaspoon salt

Combine your jam, egg, milk and butter in a mixing bowl; mix well. Sift together dry ingredients; beat them into the first mixture. Oil a muffin pan and pour the mixture into the cups. Use another muffin pan, if necessary. Bake at 375° for 30 minutes. Serve hot or cold with a plain lemon sauce. If you'd like, you can bake this in two layer pans, and put a layer of whipped cream between them.

1927 BREAD AND MARMALADE PUDDING

Here's an easy recipe that calls for things you will have in the house. You'll need:

6 slices of bread
Butter
Orange or any flavor
   marmalade

3 cups milk, scalded
2 eggs
¼ cup sugar
⅛ teaspoon salt

Butter the bread and spread each piece with marmalade. Cut bread into finger lengths and place in a baking dish. Beat eggs and sugar together until well blended. Add the salt and milk. Pour this mixture over the bread, and set the baking dish in a pan of hot water. (I always fill my broiler pan with hot water.) Bake at 300° until firm in the center. Serve half-warm, or cold, with or without cream.

1870 SWEET POTATO PUDDING

Although this recipe comes from a 1928 magazine, the recipe is much older. It was originally recorded in an 1870 cookbook writted by a lady named Mrs. Hill.

1 pint (2 cups) sugar
1 large spoon of butter
½ pint molasses
A pint of raw peeled sweet
   potatoes, grated

Milk
Grated orange rind
Dash of ground ginger
3 eggs, well beaten

Mix first 4 ingredients; add enough milk to make the mixture rather thin. Now season it to taste with orange rind and a touch of ginger. After this is mixed well, add 3 well beaten eggs. You'll want to bake this in a very slow oven so that it "candies" on top. Try 275° for an hour and a half and check for doneness.
Note: You might want to try some Hard Sauce with this for a special touch.

MISC. DESSERTS

1948 PEACH BUTTERCRUNCH

Some manufacturers still call margarine "oleomargarine," and some people call margarine "oleo." In 1948 both were commonplace and many states prohibited companies from coloring their products yellow. No matter, this 1948 recipe calls for neither white or yellow margarine, just these few ingredients:

Peach Cream:

2 teaspoons plain gelatin
¼ cup canned cling peach
  syrup
2 cups mashed cling peaches
¼ cup sugar

Pinch of salt
½ cup whipping cream,
  whipped
Buttercrunch (recipe follows)

Soften gelatin in peach syrup; let stand 5 minutes. For your peach cream just heat the mashed peaches, sugar, and salt to boiling; add the gelatin, stirring until dissolved. Chill until it is slightly thickened. Fold in stiffly whipped cream. Pour peach cream into well-oiled molds; chill until firm. Unmold, and surround with your butter crunch mixture.

Buttercrunch:

3 tablespoons butter	1 tablespoon all-purpose flour
½ cup firmly packed brown sugar	2 tablespoons water
	2 cups corn flakes cereal

To make the buttercrunch, melt your butter in a saucepan; add sugar and flour which you have blended together. Then add water. Stir the mixture until it has dissolved the sugar mixture. Cook to a soft ball stage. Remove from the heat, and pour over the corn flakes. Be sure and mix well, but lightly. Spread mixture in a shallow pan, and cool until ready to serve with Peach Cream.

CARAMEL CHARLOTTE RUSSE

Not too long ago I tried to remember a rich recipe I had eaten as a child. It came from one of the small, but delightful bakeries in my hometown, and it was called, a Charlotte Russe. I found, after trying to find this recipe, that there were many people who had similar memories of this delicious cake. Finally, in an old, but treasured magazine from the late twenties, I came upon this wonderful recipe for a caramel Charlotte Russe. This recipe is dedicated to all the friends this dessert has made throughout the years.

1 tablespoon unflavored gelatin	½ cup boiling water
¼ cup cold water	1½ cups evaporated milk
½ cup sugar	6 lady fingers
	Whipped cream

Soak gelatin in cold water for 5 minutes. Caramelize the sugar by cooking it in a skillet over a low flame, until browned, stirring frequently. Add boiling water slowly to it, and stir until the caramel is dissolved. Stir in gelatin and sugar until dissolved. Chill until mixture thickens slightly. Add the milk. Wet your mold, and line with lady fingers; cover with russe mixture. Chill. Serve with whipped cream.

1928 PINEAPPLE WATER ICE

My grandmother lived in a wonderful neighborhood . . . and I loved to visit her. We'd make an early morning visit to Popoff the butcher, and she'd buy some meat, and perhaps a chicken. Sometimes Popoff would let me keep the nickel-sized yellow eggs, and my grandmother would take them home and cook them for me.

After the Butcher Shop we'd go to Litvacks Grocery for fresh vegetables, and on the way home we'd stop off at the water ice man's cart. It was always parked at the same place . . . and I could choose between grape or lemon, cherry or lime. This was real water ice . . . the kind that takes hours to make and minutes to devour! Here is a recipe reminiscent of those days . . . it comes from a popular woman's magazine, and is included in a section for a Hawaiian luncheon. To make this water ice you'll need:

1 cup water	1 egg white, stiffly beaten
2 cups sugar	Rock salt
3½ cups pineapple juice	Ice

Heat water with sugar in a 2-quart saucepan to 225°. Stop stirring when the sugar dissolves, and boil vigorously for about 5 minutes. Remove from heat and add the pineapple juice. Chill. When it's cold, pour it into a mold or ice cream freezer, and pack in equal parts of ice and salt for 2 hours. Fold in a stiffly beaten egg white, and repack for another 1½ hours.

1921 JAM FRUIT BETTY

Everyone has heard of Brown Betty, but how many of us have ever experimented with something other than the usual apples? This recipe has apples all right, but it also includes pineapple, rhubarb, or orange marmalade, as desired.

2 tablespoons butter
2 cups chopped apples
½ cup pineapple, rhubarb, or
   orange marmalade

3 cups soft bread crumbs
Ground nutmeg
Light brown sugar

Oil your baking dish with vegetable oil or part of your butter. Stir the apples and marmalade together; set aside. Put a layer of crumbs in the baking dish, then cover with some of the apple and marmalade mixture. Top with a little nutmeg and light brown sugar, depending on the size of your dish, you might have enough to make another layer of each. Bake at 350° for 45 minutes. Serve with hard sauce.

1924 JELLIED GINGER PEARS

2 tablespoons unflavored
   gelatin
¼ cup cold water
½ cup boiling water
½ cup sugar
½ cup orange juice
3 tablespoons lemon juice

½ cup pear syrup
1 cup ginger ale
4 canned pears, cut in strips
Whipped cream
¼ cup chopped crystallized
   ginger

First you'll want to soften the gelatin in cold water for 5 minutes. Dissolve gelatin mixture in boiling water. Stir in sugar, fruit juices, and ginger ale. Chill until mixture begins to stiffen. Fold in pears. Turn this mixture into a pretty mold, and chill until firm. Serve with whipped cream and chopped ginger. Serves 8.

1922 PEACHES FROZEN IN CREAM

In 1922 Dodge was known as Dodge Brothers, an Essex cost $1295, and a Hudson Coach $1625. Pipeless furnaces were new on the market and began at $52.95. In America's kitchens, everything was "just peachy."

1 cup sugar
2 cups water
3 egg yolks, beaten until light
2 cups cream

½ teaspoon vanilla extract
½ teaspoon almond extract
1 cup sliced fresh or frozen
   peaches

Boil the sugar and water for about 5 minutes. Gradually pour water mixture over beaten egg yolks, beating constantly. Pour this mixture into the top of a double-boiler and beat over boiling water for two minutes. Now place the top of the double-boiler into a bowl of cold water and beat until it turns cold. Add your cream, and flavoring, and freeze to a mush in three parts ice to one part salt. Stir in the peaches and freeze until solid.

1923 MOCK POACHED EGGS (A DESSERT!)

This is a cake dessert, not an egg dish. The reason for the name is the visual results, which resembles poached eggs. This is a quick dessert that tastes great! You'll need:

Sponge cake or any kind of
   light cake
1 small can of peach halves
   (you can substitute
   apricots)

Whipped cream

Cut a good-sized square of cake, and place on a dessert plate. On top of this place a peach or apricot half, rounded side up. Pour about a spoonful of the peach syrup over this. Now border the cake with whipped cream to look like egg white. Repeat this for each piece of cake you serve.

1924 APPLES ALLEGRETTI

Here's an easy-to-make dessert that calls for good things like nuts, apples, raisins, and chocolate.

4 tart apples (uniform in size and shape)
¾ cup chopped nuts and raisins
½ cup cold water

1 cup powdered sugar
Lukewarm water
1 teaspoon vanilla extract
1 square unsweetened chocolate, melted

Wash and core the apples. Put them in an oven-to-table baking dish, and cover with cold water. Bake slowly at 250° until tender. (Do not let them lose their shape.) Fill the center of each apple with chopped nuts and raisins, and when the apples are done and cool cover them with a frosting made from powdered sugar and a little lukewarm water along with vanilla. When cold and firm, coat the apples with the melted chocolate.

Smooth Puddings

When you are making any kind of pudding or pie filling which calls for sugar and flour or cornstarch, if you will mix the sugar and flour or sugar and cornstarch together before mixing them with the other ingredients, your product will always be smooth.

1920 RASPBERRY CREAM WHIP

Everything in this unusual dessert is delicious, so there's not much to go wrong. We don't think to use raspberries very often, and it's a shame. You'll see why after this. As I said earlier, when this recipe was first published, there were no such things as miniature marshmallows, and one had to cut their marshmallows into bite-sized pieces. If you really want to be authentic, do the same.

1½ cups canned raspberries	½ cup heavy cream
1 cup miniature marshmallows	¼ cup walnuts or pecans

Combine raspberries and marshmallows; let stand in a cold place in your refrigerator. Now, whip your cream til stiff. When the raspberry mixture is well chilled, fold in whipped cream. Stir in nuts. Garnish with pieces of marshmallow. Chill until serving time. You may want to add a little sugar to your whipping cream, depending on your sweet tooth.

Confections

Confections

MOLASSES TAFFY

1 cup molasses
¾ cup sugar
2 teaspoons vinegar

1 tablespoon butter
⅛ teaspoon baking soda
⅛ teaspoon salt

Combine the molasses, sugar and vinegar in a heavy saucepan; boil to the hard ball stage (265° to 270°). Remove from your fire and add the butter, baking soda and salt; stir just enough to blend. Pour mixture into a well-buttered pan, and let cool. When the taffy is cool, pull it until light and porous and cut into 1″ pieces. Wrap or just serve as is.

1932 VINEGAR TAFFY

If it came from Europe—it was better. That was the general feeling about beauty products and fashion advice. Magazine ads featured skin specialists from Vienna, and perfumes and gowns from Paris. While we poured through pages of our favorite magazines, we devoured this lemon-crystal taffy, which was brittle and had a faint lemon taste, though there was no lemon in it.

2 cups sugar
½ cup vinegar
Pinch of salt

⅛ teaspoon cream of tartar
2 tablespoons butter

Combine all ingredients and boil to the hard ball stage (265° to 270°). Pour into a well-buttered pan and cool. Now comes the fun! Pull your taffy until it becomes white and porous. Then cut into 1″ pieces.

1932 PULLED MINTS

This recipe is also from 1932, when long distance calls cost 25¢ for 25 miles and Del Monte was in the coffee business. Junket was a favorite dessert and pulled mints were an extra special treat the whole family could make together.

2 cups sugar	½ teaspoon peppermint
1 cup water	flavoring
4 tablespoons butter	Powdered sugar

Combine 2 cups sugar, water, and butter together in a heavy sauce-pan; boil to the hard ball stage (265° to 270°). Remove from heat and add flavoring. Pour mixture into a well buttered pan and pull until mixture is brittle. Cut into 1" pieces and place in a dish of powdered sugar. Leave them there until the mints become creamy.

1914 BUTTERSCOTCH

This 1914 recipe is fun to make because it is easy, and also something you can come up with on the spur of the moment. You should have all of these ingredients in your pantry now.

½ cup firmly packed brown sugar	¼ cup butter
	2 teaspoons vinegar
½ cup sugar	½ capful vanilla extract
½ cup water	

Combine all of your ingredients, except the vanilla, in a saucepan. Cook until mixture begins to boil. Cover the saucepan and boil without stirring until mixture reaches the soft crack stage (275° to 280°). Remove from heat and add vanilla. DON'T STIR! Pour quickly into a well-buttered pan. It should be in a thin sheet. Cool just slightly and mark in squares.

1941 MARZIPAN

Marzipan has always fascinated me. I recently saw the most beautiful cake with decorations of marzipan. When I went to purchase ready-made marzipan fruits, I found them to be very expensive. This 1941 recipe makes a good deal of the candy, and besides costing less, is fun to make.

1 pound blanched almonds
1 pound confectioners sugar
3 tablespoons cold water
½ teaspoon almond extract
1 teaspoon rose water
Food coloring

Whole cloves
8 ounces dipping chocolate
   (optional)
Pitted dates, candied orange
   peel

Grind the almonds in your blender, and mix them with the sugar, water, almond extract and rose water. Knead the mixture until it becomes firm and smooth. You can add more water if necessary. Wrap in wax paper and store in a cool place. Color your marzipan whatever colors you wish, but leave the largest portion white. Mold the marzipan into the shapes you want and stuff the dates with marzipan as well. You can make "potatoes" by shaping the marzipan into irregular balls, using toothpicks to make depressions, and then making eyes with slivered almonds and rolling in dry cocoa. This 1941 recipe popped up as a brand new idea in a recent issue of a popular gourmet magazine! You can use the cloves to make realistic stems for pears or apples. And you can dip the marzipan in chocolate for an extra treat. Decorate with orange peel, candies or other nuts.

1928 RAISIN CREAM FUDGE

Oh doesn't it sound delicious! And it is.

2 cups sugar
⅔ cup light cream
1 tablespoon butter or
  margarine

1 teaspoon vanilla extract
½ cup seedless raisins

Get out a saucepan and put the sugar and cream in. Cook slowly, stirring until the sugar has dissolved. Stop stirring, but continue cooking until a soft ball is formed when a little of the syrup is dropped into cold water (about 238° F.). Remove from heat and add your butter. When the whole thing has cooled, add the vanilla, and beat until creamy. Stir in raisins at the last; pour mixture into a buttered pan. When it becomes firm you can cut into squares and serve.

1940 CRYSTALLIZED ROSE PETALS

Back in 1940 a curious gardener set out to find a way to eat the fragrant and beautiful roses he grew. He found the answer in an old cookbook. By crystallizing the petals like you do with orange rind, he got an unusual confection.

1 pound rose petals
1 pound sugar

Water

Choose red or pink rose petals one by one until you have a pound. Put the flowers in water and let it drain off while you make a fine sugar syrup, equal in amount to the flowers. Put the rose petals in the syrup and let the mixture boil up 5 or 6 times. Then remove it from the fire, and let it stand until the sugar forms a coating around the flowers. Drain the excess syrup off, and separate each petal so they will dry. Keep in a cool, dry place. You can do this with Parma violets too.

CRYSTALLIZED ROSE PETALS #2

I have to admit that the taste of rose petals didn't exactly thrill me. I offer these two rose petal recipes because they were a part of the times. But I wouldn't suggest you count on them to thrill and excite your friends.

Dark red roses, highly scented   **1 egg**
                                      Sugar

Wash your rose petals well, and remove the white pulp from the base of each petal. Separate your egg and save the yolk for another time. Beat the white til it foams. Then dip your pastry brush in it and brush both sides of the rose petal. You can use your fingers if you like. They should be moist only. But be sure that no excess egg white remains as it will make the petals shrivel. Shake sugar on both sides of the petal and put them on a tray to dry in your refrigerator.

CONFECTIONS

1928 SALTED NUTS

We take things like colored sheets for granted now-a-days, but in 1928 they were a new decorating idea that really excited the public. Women wore silk stockings and corsets. Toasters now had controls and everyone felt quite modern. But salted nuts had yet to hit the market and if you wanted them, you had to make them.

This is a fun way of cooking up something special. You can use any kind of nut, but for demonstration purposes we'll use almonds. Pour your almonds into boiling water and blanch them, making sure your kettle is large enough to let the nuts move about freely. When they float, they are about ready for draining. And you can take them off the burner. Let the nuts stay in the hot water until the shells slip off easily with only light pressure from your fingers. You can test this as soon as the nuts float and the skins are nice and plump. Sometimes, if you let them soak too long, they become water logged. If this should happen just spread them out on a baking sheet and let them dry in a slow (225°) oven until crisp. When they are ready to salt, they should be white, tender, and brittle.

Pour them into a sieve to drain as soon as they are ready to be taken from the water. Drain thoroughly. Allow the steam to escape by shaking up and down several times. When you have done this, toss them into a towel and take the skins off.

You can do this by taking hold of both ends of the towel and picking up handfuls of the nuts at the same time and rubbing them between your thumb and fingers. They should slip off easily if they are well drained. Now heat about a quarter of an inch of olive oil in a frying pan. When the oil looks like it is moving but it hasn't smoked yet, add the nuts. Just fry two or three tablespoons-full of nuts at a time and make sure they are well immersed in oil. Keep them in constant motion and brown them evenly. It only takes a minute or two to cook them, so watch what you're doing!! Take the nuts from the oil while they are a little lighter than you want them to be when they are done. You see, oil holds the heat, and

174

they will continue to brown even after they are removed from the fire. Drain them well over the frying pan, and then spread them over paper towels and sprinkle with salt while the oil on the outside of nut is still hot. No loose salt should cling to them!

1928 CLEAR LOLLYPOPS AND DROPS

In 1928 the film industry was turned upside down with the likes of the vitaphone, Movietone, and Phototone. "Silents" were on their way out, and teachers of elocution, voice, and culture were doing a booming business. Tenors were popping up successfully everywhere. And everywhere you went people were talking about talking pictures. Back in their kitchens, with no television to watch on a Saturday night, the family was making candy together. Here are some of those 1928 recipes:

Clear Drops:

1½ cups sugar
⅓ cup light corn syrup
⅛ teaspoon cream of tartar
¾ cup water

10 drops of flavoring (today, the choices are endless)
Food coloring

Slowly boil the sugar, corn syrup, cream of tartar, and water together without stirring, until it reaches 310°. Remove from the fire, and add your flavoring and food coloring. There are some wonderful flavors available today such as caramel, maple, and black cherry. You can find them at gourmet and specialty stores everywhere. After adding the food coloring, shape the mixture into drops, or lollypops, or, if you have candy molds, use them to form molded candy.

*This chart was taken from a 1924 magazine, now defunct.
It can still be referred to today.*

MEASURE THE DAILY FOOD HABITS OF YOUR FAMILY BY THIS SCORE-CARD

	PERFECT SCORE	GOOD SCORE
Milk		
One quart daily for children under twenty years	20	
One pint daily for adults over twenty years		
One pint daily for children under twenty years		
Three-fourths pint daily for adults over twenty years		15
Vegetables (*in addition to potatoes*)		
Two or more servings daily	15	
One serving daily		10
If two or more servings weekly are greens, add	5	5
Fruit		
Two or more servings daily	15	
One serving daily		10
If one or more servings daily are fresh fruit or tomatoes (canned or fresh), add	5	5
Cereals (*including bread, breakfast cereals and flours*)		
One-half or more of all cereals in the form of whole cereal	15	
At least one-third of all the cereals in the form of whole cereal		10
Cheese, Eggs, Meat (*including fish and poultry*)		
One serving of any two of the above daily	15	
One serving of any one of the above daily		10
Water		
One and one-half quarts or more of liquid daily	10	
One quart of liquid daily		5
Total credits	___	___
For each of the following undesirable habits deduct five: Tea or coffee for children; over two cups of tea or coffee or both for adults daily; eating sweets between meals		
Total deductions	___	___
Total score	═══	═══

Sauces

Sauces

1927 TUTTI FRUITY SAUCE

Remember when you could buy soup for 12¢ a can? It was the same year that Richard Barthelmeiss starred in "The Patent Leather Kid," and the "Heatarola" turned parlors into living-rooms. This 1927 recipe makes plain ice cream into something special.

1 cup sugar
½ cup water
¼ cup raisins
¼ cup candied cherries

½ cup figs
¼ cup chopped walnuts
¼ cup macaroon crumbs

Boil your sugar and water together for 5 minutes. Put the raisins, cherries, and figs through a food chopper or blend until finely chopped. Add fruit to the sugar mixture; cook for 3 minutes. Cool. When the mixture is slightly cooler, add your walnuts and macaroon crumbs and serve over vanilla ice cream.

1920 HARD SAUCE

Here's a Hard Sauce the way I like it . . . without any alcohol or alcohol flavoring. You might like to add your own rum flavoring. For this magazine's recipe you'll need:

⅓ cup butter
1 cup sifted powdered sugar

Flavoring, if you choose

Cream the butter until light; gradually add the powdered sugar, beating until fluffy. Add the flavoring; beat well.

1928 RICE WITH FRUIT SAUCE

Cook your favorite kind of rice, be it instant, or long grain, and then top with this fruity sauce.

Cold water
⅓ cup dried apricots
⅓ cup chopped dates ·
⅓ cup puffed raisins, cut up

4 teaspoons cornstarch
1 cup sugar
2 cups boiling water
1 tablespoon lemon juice

Pour cold water into a bowl and soak the apricots in it. Drain, and cut the apricots into pieces. Combine apricots, dates and raisins, and set aside. Combine cornstarch and sugar in a double-boiler or heavy enameled pan; add boiling water, stirring constantly. Cook until thickened and clear. (Be sure and stir constantly to avoid lumping and burning.) Add your fruit, and continue cooking for 10 minutes. Just before serving add the lemon juice. Serve over cooked rice for a great variation on an old theme.

1947 COFFEE WHIPPED CREAM

2 teaspoons sugar
1 cup heavy cream

1 to 2 teaspoons instant coffe
granules

Add 2 teaspoons of sugar and 1 cup of heavy cream to 1 to 2 teaspoons of instant coffee; beat until stiff enough to mound. Serve over desserts of all kinds.

1933 MAYONNAISE

Remember when you could mail a letter for 3¢? The year was 1933, the same year you could try out some of the newer appliances. You might think automatic defrosting refrigerators are fairly new, but in 1933 there were several models on the market. There were some other pretty modern ideas being showcased . . . things like washable wallpaper, and swinging faucets. Most of us were busy at home with our oil stoves, however, cooking all kinds of things to make life more pleasant. If we had electric mixers, this recipe was a cinch, and required no cooking at all.

1 egg
2 tablespoons lemon juice or
   vinegar
1 teaspoon dry mustard

1 teaspoon salt
1 teaspoon sugar
Dash of pepper
2 cups oil

Mix the egg, lemon juice, mustard, salt and sugar, along with the pepper, together in your electric mixer bowl. Gradually add the oil, and blend well. Refrigerate.

EGGLESS MAYONNAISE

I've given you one recipe for traditional mayonnaise. Now here's one you can make if you have a problem with eggs. It comes from a 1920 magazine that features an ad for an evaporated milk. A portion of the advertisement for this milk tells you that if the iceman fails to come, and your regular milk sours, you can use your evaporated milk. Aren't you glad the iceman doesn't cometh any more?!
For eggless mayonnaise you'll need:

½ teaspoon salt
¼ teaspoon dry mustard
¼ teaspoon pepper
3 tablespoons undiluted
　evaporated milk

¾ cup salad oil
2 tablespoons sharp vinegar

Combine all of your seasonings and add your milk. Now gradually beat in the oil with your beater. Whip in the vinegar, and put in a jar! If it gets too thick, you can thin it out by just adding a little more evaporated milk.

P.S. Want to make a Russian Dressing? Add to your eggless mayonnaise:

1 chopped hard cooked egg
¼ cup chili sauce
1 tablespoon minced pimentos

1 tablespoon minced parsley
1½ tablespoons minced chives
　or onion

Stir well, and chill until serving time.